Social Networks and Marketing

RELEVANT KNOWLEDGE SERIES

Social Networks and Marketing

CHRISTOPHE VAN DEN BULTE
STEFAN WUYTS

MARKETING SCIENCE INSTITUTE
Cambridge, Massachusetts

Contents

Foreword

In Summer 2006, the trustees of MSI cast their biennial votes for the new MSI research priorities. "The connected customer" emerged as the central theme around which several research agendas were advanced. Customers are connected to each other, to their suppliers, and to independent third parties in new and unparalleled ways. These connections change customer behavior in fundamental ways, and thus open new opportunities as well as challenges for the practice of marketing.

The framework par excellence to study the connected customer is the social network paradigm. This is the subject of the sixth monograph in MSI's highly successful Relevant Knowledge Series, written by two leading academics in this area, Christophe Van den Bulte of the University of Pennsylvania and Stefan Wuyts of Tilburg University, The Netherlands.

Christophe Van den Bulte and Stefan Wuyts introduce a new vocabulary, indeed a new way of thinking about marketing and its impact on prospects and customers. These concepts, as well as the models that connect them to each other, will help the marketing professional of the 21st century better understand and manage the world of social contagion, buzz marketing, viral marketing, and a host of related phenomena that have become so relevant in both B2C and B2B markets.

Social Networks and Marketing could not have been more timely, and we are grateful to Christophe and Stefan for their contribution.

Dominique M. Hanssens
UCLA
MSI Executive Director, 2005-07

Introduction

Social networks are everywhere in the marketer's world. Consumers share information about products. Some brand aficionados even band together in vibrant brand communities. Product managers mobilize the support of multiple colleagues scattered through the corporation to develop and launch new products. Communication managers know that word-of-mouth can give a wonderful boost to their campaigns' ROI. Salespeople appreciate the value of the opinion leaders in their territory or vertical segment. Business development managers and entrepreneurs know that the most novel ideas tend to come through references outside their regular set of contacts. At the corporate level, executives keen to keep their firm efficient yet nimble learn to view their organizations as constellations of people, technologies, and hard assets.

Though ubiquitous for centuries, social networks have become a hot topic among marketing practitioners only recently, as emerging information technologies facilitate communication among consumers, among colleagues, and among firms. The question of how the pattern of interconnections among social entities—consumers, colleagues, business units, competitors, or complementors—affects behaviors and outcomes of those entities is now receiving more attention than ever before.

The purpose of this monograph is to provide a primer on social networks targeted toward marketing practitioners and scholars. It presents the main concepts, theoretical ideas, and empirical findings of interest to marketing. The focus is on substantive ideas rather than methodology. Unlike the previous monographs in MSI's Relevant Knowledge Series, many of the ideas and findings reviewed here stem from outside the marketing discipline. Despite their ubiquity and relevance, social networks have long been ignored in marketing science and education. We hope this slender volume effectively spans the structural hole between the ideas and findings developed by social network analysts and economic sociologists and the issues of interest to marketers. Thus, while *Social Networks and Marketing* is a broad title for so small a book, it succinctly describes the scope of our endeavor.

We begin by addressing the question, "Why should marketers care about social networks?" We explore the developments in the business environment that are prompting managers to look into social network analysis. We then offer a conceptual "toolkit" of social network concepts, and discuss the idea of "social capital," i.e., how particular positions in networks can confer particular benefits. In the next three chapters, we review empirical research on consumer, intra-organizational, and inter-organizational networks. Our focus is on answering questions relevant to managers: How and when do network patterns matter? How does network structure affect behaviors and outcomes of actors, both inside and outside the firm? What kinds of social networks are relevant for which types of marketing decisions? We conclude with an assessment of the current state of knowledge and with a discussion of research challenges and opportunities.

Christophe Van den Bulte
Stefan Wuyts

Social Networks and Marketing

1

Why Should Marketers Care about Social Networks?

What Franklin, Carnegie, and Edison Knew

Entrepreneurs and other business people have long appreciated the importance of social networks. Benjamin Franklin, for instance, was a master at leveraging his connections with fellow entrepreneurs, scientists, and politicians. He even organized groups in which people of different backgrounds and expertise educated each other on novel ideas and developments (Franklin 2005). Today, social network analysts would call such groups an application of "cross-cutting social circles" and "bridging through weak ties" in the area of "knowledge management." Andrew Carnegie, Jay Gould, and John Pierpont Morgan also used social connections to their benefit, and social networks continue to play a critical role in modern finance (e.g., Eccles and Crane 1988; Laird 2006; Mizruchi and Stearns 2001).

Scientists and engineers are keenly aware of the importance of social networks in generating new ideas as well as in mobilizing resources to develop them into technologies (e.g., Allen 1977; Latour 1987). In fact, social networks have been critical to those operating at the intersection of science and finance for centuries. Thomas Edison, for instance, mobilized the resources of co-workers and their families beyond his own financial and patent-based resources to create the company that later became General Electric. He and his associate Samuel Insull also exploited antagonisms among financiers to raise additional funding—which social network analysts today would call an application of the "structural balance" principle in networks in order to achieve "network leverage" (McGuire, Granovetter, and Schwartz 1993).

Like financiers, scientists, and entrepreneurs, marketers have long recognized the importance of social networks, but to a more limited extent. In general, marketers have focused on the role of opinion leadership and contagion processes in new product diffusion, an area of research that has made little progress within marketing since it developed in the 1960s and early 1970s. A few practitioners have exploited social networks in more marginal, even disreputable, ways, as in party selling and direct selling organizations like Amway.[1] Finally, while relationship marketing in consumer and business markets has received ample attention from marketing academics, it has been seen in dyadic terms rather than in a network context (Iacobucci and Hibbard 1999).

In short, while not totally ignored, social networks have not been recognized as an important issue in marketing. Much of that is changing. In the last five years, marketing practitioners' interest in social networks has surged dramatically. Several developments in the business environment, and in academia, have prompted this shift. We discuss these below.

Social Networks and Marketing Today

Eroding Effectiveness of Traditional Marketing The decline in effectiveness of mass media may be the primary reason for B2C marketers' renewed interest in social networks today. Media fragmentation caused by an ever-increasing number of magazines, radio stations, television channels, and websites may be a boon for firms catering to specialized needs of micro-segments but is a bane for firms targeting products of general appeal toward the mass market (Turow 1997). Another trend is consumers' deepening skepticism of advertising and marketing. Increasingly, consumers, in particular teenagers, view marketing efforts as schemes and try to see through the "schemers' schemas" (Friestad and Wright 1994, 1995). As traditional marketing communication becomes less effective, marketers are turning to new means of communication capitalizing on consumers' social networks to convey their message.

B2B marketers are also concerned about decreasing returns on their marketing efforts. Many feel that managers and other decision makers in customer organizations have less time to listen to sales pitches after years of downsizing, de-layering, and re-engineering. Similarly, several pharmaceutical firms believe that physicians are now saturated with sales calls, and are trying to complement or even partially replace their traditional detailing and direct marketing with various forms of word-of-mouth marketing.

Networks' Relevance to Branding Efforts Building and managing one's brands and corporate reputation has become a top management priority in recent years. From a cognitive psychology perspective, a brand can be thought of as a node in one's memory that is linked with other beliefs through ties of varying strengths, i.e., as a node in an associative network (Keller 2002). Many of the tools developed to analyze social networks of interconnected social actors (individuals, departments, firms, countries, etc.) can be used to study associative networks and develop useful brand diagnostics. For example, Henderson, Iacobucci, and Calder (1998, 2002) use social network analysis tools to shed light on branding issues including branded features, driver brands, complements, co-branding, cannibalization, brand parity, brand dilution, brand confusion, counter-brands, and segmentation.

Research in economic sociology demonstrates that firms' networks of ties to other firms and institutions can imbue them with high or low prestige and with strong or weak reputations for quality. Similar to co-branding ties between brands, social network ties between firms can act as a proxy for unobserved quality—with effects strong enough to affect profit margins and market shares (Podolny 2005).

Connecting Brands to Consumers Marketers are increasingly interested in how consumers use products and brands to build and maintain a social identity. This symbolic use of products and brands does not occur in a social vacuum; rather, consumers use them as bridges toward or fences against other people (Douglas and Isherwood 1979). Understanding the patterns of positive and negative connections among customers may help marketers in their segmentation, targeting, positioning, and marketing communication, as brands like Red Bull, Vans, and Diesel Jeans illustrate.

One specific tactic that has attracted much attention lately is to allow and even facilitate the creation and sharing of consumer-generated (rather than firm-generated) content. This, the argument goes, may result in stronger and deeper connections between brands and consumers and more effective brand communities. This hope appears to fuel the interest of a number of large fast-moving consumer-goods companies in social networking sites like MySpace, Facebook, Cyworld, and Bebo and video sharing sites like YouTube. Ironically, social network theory and research do not have much guidance to offer in this regard, for two reasons. First, it is not clear to what extent many of these sites are based on networking principles. Many members seem to use them as a platform to express themselves and check out others, i.e., as a platform for exhibitionism and voyeurism. Second, marketers currently treat these sites primarily as a new channel to reach teenagers rather than as networks in which the pattern or structure of ties is of interest. A better understanding of network concepts and tools, however, might offer marketers new approaches to leverage the potential of such sites to act as true social networks.

Global Marketing Challenges As Western firms look to emerging markets to sustain their growth, their marketers face challenges posed by the lack of a strong marketing services industry, the lack of brand heritage, and the question of how to fit products and brands into existing consumption patterns. A social network perspective may help marketers find effective solutions to these problems. For example, engaging in more word-of-mouth marketing would presumably be effective in cultures that are more collectivist, more uncertainty avoiding, and more status-sensitive than Western cultures (for indirect evidence, see Van den Bulte and Stremersch 2004). A study of credit card marketing in Russia (see sidebar) offers another example of how marketers can leverage social networks in emerging markets (Guseva 2005; Guseva and Rona-Tas 2001).

Credit card marketing in Russia

One of the most important problems credit cards companies face is uncertainty about the creditworthiness of cardholders. This problem is magnified in newly emerging or developing economies which lack the infrastructure of credit rating agencies and scoring models based on financial history. Russian banks have used network-based strategies to manage that uncertainty. Initially, they simply hand-picked cardholders from their managers' personal social networks or from among political and cultural elites. Direct social ties or individuals' high status facilitated pre-screening and monitoring customers, and limited delinquency by the potential for poor payers to be shamed among their peers. In short, networks helped in recruiting customers and instilling financial discipline. However, the pool of prospects this strategy offered was limited to the upper and upper-middle classes, and was exhausted rather rapidly. In the mid 1990s, Russian banks began a new strategy in which they made agreements with enterprises to supply all their employees with cards, secured by their salaries directly deposited to the bank. In this arrangement, enterprises were "middlemen" that provided banks with imme-diate access to thousands of individual customers and also frequently served as guarantors on overdrafts. In short, banks found critical nodes in the network they could use as leverage points to gain access to many more customers and who, in addition, provided third-party guarantees in case of delinquency.

The strategies used by the Russian banks illustrate key concepts in social net-work theory that we will cover in detail in later chapters.[2] This example makes clear how the underlying ideas and mechanisms of social networks are likely to offer solutions to marketing challenges in emerging economies when more formal mar-ket information providers and communication channels are not available.

New Products and Innovation Firms have long tried to exploit social networks to improve their ability to understand, forecast, and manage how new products dif-fuse through the marketplace. In the 1960s, firms turned to new theories of opin-ion leadership, two-step flow, and social contagion over social networks (Katz and Lazarsfeld 1955; Shaw 1965). In the 1990s, high-tech marketers turned to a variant on those ideas that similarly emphasized the importance of carefully targeting one's customers with a view of leveraging them to gain yet other customers (Moore 1991). It is clear that social network theory has much to offer marketers in this area.

Complementary Network Effects A key issue that marketers of many, though not all, IT products face is the presence of complementary network effects. This is the phenomenon where the value of a product to the customer increases with the number of other customers who have bought or are using the product itself or its complements.

These network effects are "direct" when the utility of using a product increases with the installed base of that same product (as with point-to-point communication devices like fax machines or product categories where users share objects such as computer spreadsheets and videogames). Direct complementary network effects can lead to strong imitation dynamics among users, resulting in explosive growth once a critical level of installed base has been reached, a phenomenon sometimes referred to as "excess momentum." However, these direct effects can also lead many consumers to defer their adoption until they are certain that the product's installed base will be large enough for them to extract enough value out of the product. This phenomenon, which slows down initial adoption and hence lengthens the payback period on one's investments, is sometimes referred to as "excess inertia."[3]

Complementary network effects are "indirect" when the utility of using a product (say, a piece of hardware like a Blu-Ray DVD player) depends on the installed base, or at least on the ready availability, of complements (say, software like movie titles). Such indirect effects also create strong imitation dynamics among consumers, and marketers must ensure that both their product and its complements are marketed effectively. Firms must either enter the complement business (through internal development or acquisition), or coordinate their efforts with other suppliers and possibly with downstream systems integrators as well.

It is important to note that, while these direct or indirect complementary network effects are primarily seen in the IT industry, the underlying issue—the presence of competing standards—is not specific to IT products. The early days of the automobile industry before the current "dominant design" emerged amply illustrate this. A more current example is that the acceptance by consumers of cars using fuel cell technology will hinge in part on the ready availability of service stations suitably equipped for such cars.

The importance of complementary network effects is, in our experience, one reason why managers are eager to know more about social networks. That makes sense on the supply side, that is, when one is thinking about mobilizing support among supplier firms; however, we believe that using social networks to gain insight into complementary network effects on the demand side is rarely worth the effort. The reason is that the key factor driving customers' utility is the total installed base, and the fraction of users in each customer's own network is only marginally more relevant. Take the example of fax machines: a firm will care mostly about the installed base among its own suppliers and customers, but will also want to be available to all its future potential suppliers and customers, as well as its bank, its accounting and legal firms, and so on. Those firms' adoptions, in turn, will be driven by the adoptions of all the organizations they themselves may interact with in the future. The same again holds true for those latter organizations. So, the relevant set of potential adopters is so broad that ignoring the structure of ties and just looking at the total installed base is likely to be sufficient. Some exceptions are possible, of course, especially for very complex products or services in industrial markets where winning one or two key reference accounts can have a dispropor-tional snowball effect. (We discuss the issue of opinion leadership in Chapter 4.)

"No Business Is an Island" Marketers' recent interest in networks also stems from a broader intellectual shift. Over the last two decades, firms and scholars have come to recognize the potential benefits of long-term buyer-supplier relations, not sim-ply due to switching costs that make it prohibitive to sever the business tie, but also due to actual cooperation (e.g., Arndt 1979; Matthyssens and Van den Bulte 1994). More recently, attention has shifted from the pros and cons of such close dyadic ties between pairs of firms to those of the broader network or eco-system in which firms operate. Put differently, attention has shifted from "relational embeddedness" to "structural embeddedness" (Granovetter 1992). Many of the early ideas were based on business practices in Asia and Europe (e.g., Gerlach 1992; Håkansson and Snehota 1989; Johanson and Mattsson 1994), but American business marketers have come to recognize how they too operate within networks of suppliers, cus-tomers, regulators, and so on.

New product development is a case in point. Many firms in knowledge-intensive industries recognize that their innovativeness is strongly affected by the composi-tion of their network of partners (Powell, Koput, and Smith-Doerr 1996; Wuyts, Dutta, and Stremersch 2004), and marketers now recognize external R&D as a crit-ical issue in new product development (Wind and Mahajan 1997). This raises a number of questions for managers: "Are some network constellations better than others, and how does ours measure up?" and "How can we change or mobilize our network to our ends?" Existing theory and research on "social capital," that is, those aspects of social structure that can be used by firms and individuals to realize their interests, provide some ways for managers to address those questions.

Leveraging Knowledge Just as firms can be seen as actors within networks of organizations, they can be seen as networks themselves—of people, ideas, and resources. This perspective has become quite popular in innovation and knowledge management; there is new appreciation for the insight from Dalton (1955) and others that the organizational chart and formal information systems only partly reflect "who knows what" within the firm and that they may even be an impedi-ment to mobilizing knowledge across functional silos, divisional lines, and other traditional boundaries. Social networks can aid greatly in this double search-trans-fer challenge (although ties that facilitate the search tend to impede the transfer, and vice versa, as we will discuss in later chapters). New product managers have long appreciated the importance of good relations between marketing and R&D, but even here we see a shift from the dyadic level emphasizing close relationships to the network level emphasizing the broader pattern of ties and "the company behind the chart" (Krackhardt and Hanson 1993).

Employee Networks and Services Marketing Employees have a disproportional impact on quality and customer satisfaction in service industries (Zeithaml and Parasuraman 2004). The question whether networks can help firms hire and retain better employees is hence of particular interest to service marketers. As we will discuss in Chapter 6, research finds that social networks indeed affect the firm's ability to retain satisfied employees (Krackhardt and Porter 1985, 1986), and that employees hired through network referrals may be significantly better than others (Castilla 2005; Fernandez, Castilla, and Moore 2000).

Changes in Business Academia Most academic marketing research on the topic of social networks was conducted in the 1960s and early 1970s and the field has not made much progress since, as indicated by the very small number of publications in the marketing discipline's most prestigious academic journals. Much of marketing theory is still vested in a stimulus-response mode of thinking, where "target" customers "respond" to the marketing mix and other demand-generating "stimuli" that are directed at them, hopefully with the desired "effect." This way of thinking is most dominant in the area of sales promotion, but pervades much of consumer packaged goods marketing (Neslin 2002; van Waterschoot and Van den Bulte 1992). In the early 1980s, marketing science broadened its perspective from this purely unidirectional approach to a two-way, dyadic approach. This shift was prompted by the increasing importance of the service sectors, evidence of frequent intensive two-way interaction between buyers and sellers in business markets, the increased recognition of customer satisfaction as a key issue, and the resulting insight that the ability to manage such relationships may be a key to competitive advantage (e.g., Arndt 1983; Day and Wensley 1983; Dyer and Singh 1998; Grönroos 1994; Håkansson 1982). More recently, some marketing scholars have called for further broadening that perspective from dyadically relational to explicitly network-based (e.g., Achrol and Kotler 1999; Houston et al. 2004; Iacobucci 1996).

Marketing academics, especially doctoral students, have also been responding to changes in other areas of business academia. Some prominent business schools have hired economic sociologists, several of whom are network researchers, into faculty positions in management and strategy departments. Other management and strategy academics have simply learned social network theory and methods in their attempts to better understand power dynamics, the effective management of innovation, and the design of R&D alliances. These professors, presumably, have had an impact on M.B.A. students, either directly as instructors or indirectly through the case materials they developed. Some also have had some impact on their marketing colleagues and on the latter's doctoral students.

In spite of all these developments, the amount of expertise on social networks in marketing academia and practice remains low.[4] This book is intended to help redress that situation. We begin in the next chapter by discussing basic terms and concepts of social network analysis, with particular attention to those most relevant to marketing.

2

Conceptual Toolkit

Thinking in terms of networks has great intuitive appeal to managers and social scientists. However, the use of network ideas has tended to be metaphorical rather than analytical or operational. Although metaphors are valuable in guiding one's initial thoughts and in conveying the essence of ideas, they can be frustratingly fuzzy and even misleading as guides to action (e.g., Van den Bulte 1994).

In this chapter, we present a number of key concepts that we have culled from the literature. This conceptual "toolkit" is intended to offer building blocks to more precise theories and propositions as well as operational and quantifiable metrics for managers.

We limit ourselves to those ideas that are most relevant to marketers and present and discuss concepts verbally rather than mathematically. The appendix suggests several textbooks ranging from introductory to advanced for those who want to explore more widely or delve more deeply.

In our discussion, we draw primarily on traditional social network analysis and economic sociology rather than on work in computer science, physics, biology, and other natural sciences.[5] There are two reasons for this. First, network research in the computer and natural sciences concentrates on identifying general statistical properties of massively large networks, operating at a level of abstraction far removed from most marketers' concerns. Second, social networks differ from technical, biological, and chemical networks in important ways. For example, while technical and scientific networks may have tens of thousands of "points" or "nodes," many of which have hundreds or even thousands of connections, social networks are limited by the fact that humans cannot maintain a very large number of connections requiring sizable emotional or time commitments—exactly the type of connection that is of special interest in complex knowledge sharing and social support (Amaral et al. 2000; Newman 2001). Also unlike technical or scientific networks, social networks are characterized by humans' ability to form social identities ("Who am I?" and "Who is like me?"), which in turn influences information search since someone similar to you may be more or less useful, depending on the type of information you are looking for (Watts, Dodds, and Newman 2002). Two additional issues that further limit one's ability to generalize from nonhuman to human networks (although evidence is admittedly still more suggestive than conclusive) are that humans exhibit more "transitivity" in their connections (discussed on pages 17-18) and that they tend to be connected to others with a similar number of contacts. The opposite applies to technical and biological networks (Newman 2002; Newman and Park 2003).

Before we start laying out the conceptual tools that one can use to understand the pattern or structure of a network, let us first address a basic question. What is a social network?

Defining Social Networks

A network consists of two things: a set of discrete entities (called nodes) and the collection of ties among them. Graphically, that corresponds to a set of points and the collection of lines among them. The older literature uses the word "sociogram" for the graphical representation of a social network with nodes shown as points or bullets and ties shown as lines. Other terms used by mathematicians are "graphs" for networks, "vertices" (the plural of "vertex") for points or nodes, and "edges" for lines or ties.

Nodes and ties can be anything: people and friendships, firms and commercial transactions, venture capitalists and investing in the same venture, patents and citations to precedents, Web pages and hyperlinks, Internet routers and the cables that run between them, electric power generation stations and substations and the high-voltage transmission lines connecting them, components of a jet engine and their influence on each others' operation, biological organisms and who-eats-who connections ("food webs"), chemical molecules and the reactions that turn one chemical into another, neurons in a nervous system and the synaptic connections between them, and so on. As marketers, we are concerned mostly about networks consisting of social entities and ties.

A *social network* is simply a specific kind of network, one in which the nodes are social entities. The entities or nodes in a social network are often called *actors*. They can be individuals, organizations like firms or labor unions, formally defined groups like departments within a firm, or other collective social units like households or reading groups. Actors are linked to one another by social *ties*. Ties—which are also often referred to as *relations* or relationships[6]—might include the following:

- Buying and selling
- Requests for or sharing of information
- Transfers of resources like advice, emotional support, money, personnel, or rights to use patents
- Associations or affiliations, like being members of the same department or having graduated from the same college

■ Formal relations, like authority
■ Accessibility, possibly proxied by physical distance

If an actor has a tie to another actor, the latter is said to be a *neighbor*. If one looks at the network from the perspective of a specific actor, he or she is sometimes called an *ego* and any of his or her neighbors is called an *alter* ('I" and "other" in Latin). The network consisting of an ego and his or her alters and of the ties among all these actors is called an *egocentric network* or *ego-network*. In other words, each actor has an ego-network. The overall network, consisting of all actors and ties one is interested in, is sometimes called the *sociocentric network*, but most often people simply call it the network. See Figure 1 for an example. Note that actor F is not connected to anyone else, so his egocentric network consists of merely himself.

Unless one puts boundaries on a set of actors and ties, everything in the universe will be connected (at least indirectly) to everything else. Thus, one must impose clear boundaries on the network one is interested in. Obviously, the rele-

Figure 1
Network vs. Egocentric Network

A network with six actors

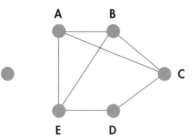

Actor A's egocentric network

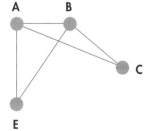

Actor E's egocentric network

vant boundaries depend on the substantive or theoretical issue one wants to address. This decision requires judgment; there is no standard rule of thumb for the "boundary specification problem," as it is sometimes called.

It is important to distinguish social networks from groups of actors. Groups are defined simply by membership based on one or more actor attributes, like demographics, prior behavior, values, and lifestyles or group membership, without taking into consideration the pattern or structure of ties among the members or between members and nonmembers. If an actor attribute is used to define a tie (e.g., "both being between 12 and 18 years of age"), network analysis does not provide any more insights than group analysis.[7] Social network analysis can address actor attributes; what sets it apart from most other types of social science research is its attention to the pattern or structure of ties among the actors. Thus, it is quite different from the traditional way marketers think about segmentation, targeting, customer lifetime value, and so on.

Properties of Ties

We now delve a little deeper into some properties of the other fundamental building block of social networks: ties. Note, a tie does not simply pertain to an individual actor; it is always part of a dyad, defined as a pair of actors and the (possible) tie(s) between them.

Directionality An important property of a tie is whether or not it is *directed* or *directional*. That is, does the tie between two actors, A and B, flow from A to B or from B to A? Angela recommending a new product to Ben (flow of advice or referral) and Brazil exporting Embraer jets to Argentina (flow of goods) are directional ties. Angela and Ben being friends, or Brazil and Argentina being trade partners, are not directional ties. If the tie is defined based on affiliation or association—such as living in the same apartment block or being members of the same trade association—it will always be nondirectional. It is also important to note that directionality matters in some respects (like opinion leadership and power), but not in others (like the opportunity for a middleman to earn nice margins through arbitrage between two actors who are not directly tied to one another).

Reciprocity and Symmetry If the tie is directional, the property of *reciprocity* or *symmetry* is important. Does the advice flow only from A to B, or is the flow reciprocal, that is, symmetric? This property is important, for example, when one wants to target opinion leaders (who tend to provide more advice than they receive) rather than simply people who are gregarious. Reciprocation is also critical for sustaining positive affect, cooperation, and trust within and across organizations

(Gouldner 1960). Generally, reciprocity implies that when A helps B, then B will help A at a later time. In some cases, this property extends outside the confines of the dyad: when A helps B, A may later receive help from B or from other actors, who are typically connected to or affiliated with B. Further, reciprocation need not be "in kind." It is a classic finding in sociology that people asking advice or help from others at work repay them with respect, not with advice or help (Blau 1955).

Multiplexity This property describes the presence of multiple kinds of relations between actors. Is the tie "multiplex" (Mitchell 1969), "multi-layered," or "multi-dimensional"? If so, the pair of actors is connected through more than one type of relation, like "asking advice from" and "paying respect to." Rather than saying that a tie between two actors is multiplex, it is often simpler to say that a pair of actors is connected in multiple kinds of networks (like advice and respect).

Strength Tie strength has attracted the most research attention in marketing, yet the concept remains somewhat nebulous. This is probably due to the fact that Granovetter's (1973) introduction of the concept proceeded from an intuitive basis and as a consequence of unexpected research findings rather than from a more a priori and formal conceptual basis. Given its importance in social network analysis, we discuss tie strength in somewhat greater detail than the other concepts.

Tie strength refers to the intensity and tightness of a tie, for example, the frequency of interaction between two people, the depth of the friendship (or animosity) between two people, and the monetary value of the trade between two firms or countries. The concept of tie strength goes beyond the presence or absence of a tie (typically represented by 0 for absent and 1 for present), to capture a more finely graded measure of its intensity and tightness.

Most analysts consider tie strength to have multiple dimensions. In a seminal article, Granovetter (1973) distinguished four dimensions but claimed these could be combined into a single concept. He defined tie strength as "a (probably linear) combination of the amount of time, the emotional intensity, the intimacy (mutual confiding), and the reciprocal services which characterize the tie." Marsden and Campbell's (1984) empirical construct validation based on three samples of interpersonal relationships provides an important insight: they find two empirically distinguishable dimensions: (1) duration and frequency (time spent in the relationship), and (2) depth (intimacy and mutual confiding). Note, intimacy and mutual confiding also connote the willingness to make oneself vulnerable to the other party, and hence should be closely related to an expectation of cooperation and to attributions of honesty and benevolence, i.e., to trust. Pretests in Frenzen and Nakamoto's (1993) study are consistent with this two-factor interpretation: they find that frequency of contact is distinct from the willingness to share personal confidences and perform favors.

In a study where 284 managers described how they saw 26 different types of relations compare to each other, Burt (1997) finds two clear underlying dimensions: frequency of contact (which he labeled "activity") and emotional closeness or "intimacy." Moreover, managers viewed these two underlying dimensions to be roughly orthogonal. This pattern is familiar in American populations (Burt 1990): people do not distinguish relations on a single dimension of strong versus weak, but on orthogonal dimensions of "activity" or "frequency" and "depth" or "closeness."

Psychologists document a similar distinction in the valence and intensity dimensions of interpersonal relationships (e.g., Wish 1976). Valence ranges from cooperative to competitive, while intensity is the extent of interdependence and, as Iacobucci and Ostrom (1996, p. 55) note, "is thought to be reflected in a variety of ways, including the frequency of dyadic interactions ... [and] the perceived commitment of the parties to the relationship." While not identical to Marsden and Campbell's distinction between depth and time spent, the distinction between valence and intensity seems a closely related way to decompose tie strength into two separate and causally more fundamental dimensions.[8]

In short, tie strength can be conceptualized as having two dimensions, which we label *tie intensity* or activity (the frequency of contact) and *tie valence* (the affective, supportive, or cooperative character of the tie). We choose the terms "tie intensity" or "tie activity" since they capture both the time spent and other resources committed. We use these terms in an emotionally neutral way, i.e., without the connotation of intimacy, vulnerability, and trust implied by "depth" and "closeness." These affective elements are captured in the second term "valence," which we chose since it is more precise than depth or closeness. This two-dimensional conceptualization of tie strength agrees best with the empirical evidence to date (in addition to the citations above, see Wellman and Wortley 1990).

As we will discuss in later chapters, the distinction between valence and intensity is important for better understanding how particular ties can help marketers achieve particular outcomes. For example, in distribution channels for complex corporate IT products, high positive valence enhances the actors' willingness to share knowledge, whereas high tie intensity enhances their ability to actually do so (Wuyts et al. 2004).

In particular settings, it may be useful to make even finer distinctions within those two dimensions. Or one may want to add duration as another tie characteristic, since it is distinct from, but often positively correlated with, valence and can enhance its effects on providing support or trust (Krackhardt 1992; Perry-Smith 2006). While it may be economical to collapse different characteristics into tie strength, one should keep in mind the multiple dimensions implied by the term.

Homophily This property is the tendency for actors to connect and mingle with other actors of their own sort. Sociologists and marketing academics studying the diffusion of new products use the term "homophily," while physicists and epidemiologists studying the spread of diseases use "assortative mixing." Both terms simply mean that similarity breeds connection (i.e., "birds of a feather flock together"), with the result that people's personal networks are homogeneous with regard to many sociodemographic, behavioral, and attitudinal characteristics. This is a surprisingly general principle that affects ties of every type, including marriage, friendship, work, advice, support, information transfer, exchange, and so on (for a detailed review, see McPherson, Smith-Lovin, and Cook [2001]).

Homophily is important because it constrains actors' social worlds. By limiting the variety of information and opinions one receives from people unlike oneself, homophily can have powerful negative impacts on learning about new ideas and products and changing one's opinions, and thus, from a marketing perspective, on new product adoption and the development of vibrant brand communities. Like Ben Franklin, whose learning circles consisted of people from different trades and walks of life, people keen to learn and stay in touch with new developments tend to be aware of this problem and to be "heterophilous" (Rogers 2003). Yet homophily can also be beneficial since it can foster trust and reciprocity. One reason is simply that it is easier to trust people who are like oneself because one feels more confident about one's ability to predict their future actions. Homophily also tends to result in densely clustered sub-networks, which helps enforce cooperative norms.

These five tie properties we have discussed—directionality, reciprocity, multiplexity, strength, and homophily—are intrinsic properties of ties and are hence relevant to simple dyads as well as broader networks. However, by increasing the set of actors from two to three or more, that is, by going from a dyad to a triad or larger network, an additional set of structural properties emerge that are intrinsic to networks rather than dyads. We discuss these below.

Some Structural Properties of Networks

In this section, we describe four structural properties of triads and larger networks: transitivity, structural balance, density, and closure (also called local clustering by physicists). Our discussion here is limited to outlining some technical-structural issues. We discuss substantive implications for cooperation, trust, the so-called "strength-of-weak-ties," and social capital in later chapters.

Transitivity A relationship is transitive if the presence of a tie from one actor (i) to a second actor (j) and from that second actor (j) to a third actor (k) also implies the presence of a tie from the first actor (i) to the third actor (k). See Figure 2. Transitivity occurs much more often than one would expect from mere chance, particularly for ties with positive affect or valence. For instance, a study analyzing

Figure 2
Some Transitive and Non-transitive Triads

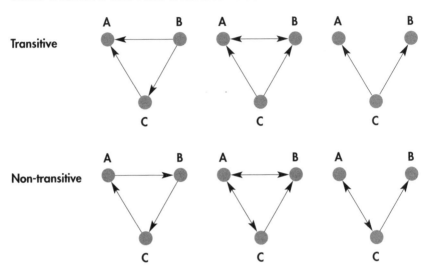

Note: Transitivity means that the following condition is met: if $i \rightarrow j$ and $j \rightarrow k$, then $i \rightarrow k$.

917 personal networks finds evidence of transitivity in an overwhelming majority of them (Holland and Leinhardt 1972). A more recent study finds that two scientists have a 30% or greater probability of collaborating if both collaborate with a common other third scientist. That is orders of magnitude higher than the base rate of collaborating with a scientist chosen at random: for a set of over 16,000 astrophysicists, the average number of collaborators is only 15; among more than 8,000 high-energy physicists, it is slightly less than 4 (Newman 2001).

Transitivity can also be found in organizational networks. Car manufacturers are more likely to have ties to suppliers of semi-finished goods (say, furniture upholstery) that do business with their supplier of components (say, car seats) than to other suppliers of semi-finished goods. A study of alliances in the global steel industry by Madhavan, Gnyawali, and He (2004) documents that firms tend to form transitive triads, in which three firms all have direct ties with each other, rather than intransitive triads, especially within blocks defined by geography or technology.

Transitivity is likely to be a driving force in how networks evolve. For instance, people often get to know each other through mutual acquaintances. The presence of a common contact B who is trusted by both A and C may act as guarantee for A and C to deepen their level of engagement with each other.

Structural Balance Structural balance is a property that is closely related to transitivity, but it is specific to ties with either positive (+) or negative (–) affect or valence. A network is structurally balanced if, when two actors like each other (+), then they are consistent in their evaluation of all other actors, and when they don't like each other (–), then they disagree in their evaluation of all others.[9] There is a quick way to check for this condition in triads: the product of all the signs must be positive. So, structural balance exists where there are three pluses ("the friends of my friends are my friends") or where there are two minuses and a plus ("the enemies of my enemies are my friends"). Other combinations are unbalanced and will lead to tension within the network, as when a strategy consulting firm tries to build a relationship with two firms that are direct competitors of each other. For example, Bain Consulting very deliberately avoids unbalanced triads, since they believe such situations decrease firms' willingness to share data and insights with consultants and hence diminish Bain's ability to provide value to their clients. Structural balance is a key driving force in the structure and evolution of human networks (e.g., see the analysis of 384 triads by Davis [1977]), and the main idea generalizes to settings where ties can be asymmetric (see the analysis of 742 small networks by Davis [1970]).

Density The density of a network is simply the proportion of actual to possible ties. For example, in a network of 5 consumers, 10 nondirectional ties can exist.[10] If the actual number of ties is 6, then network density equals 0.6 or 60%. If there are 8 ties, network density equals 0.8. While the absolute value for network density is not very informative, comparison across networks provides insight into relatively dense versus relatively sparse networks.

Closure and Local Clustering Closure, the key concept in Coleman's theory of social capital (1988, 1990) which we discuss in Chapter 3, is the density among those in a network with whom an actor has a tie. The amount of closure in a particular actor's ego-network can be operationalized as follows: If A has nondirected ties to 6 others, then a maximum of $6 \times (6 - 1) / 2 = 15$ nondirected ties are possible among those six other actors. If the number of ties among them is 15, then density in that subset of actors is 100% and closure is total; if it is 3, then density in the subset is only 20% and closure is low. This operationalization of closure is identical to what Newman, Barabási, and Watts (2006) call "local clustering."[11] One could also operationalize closure in a more expansive fashion (e.g., Coleman 1988) and consider neighbors as being "connected" not only when they share a direct tie but also when they are linked indirectly through a very short path (say, with one intermediary).

Closure tends to increase with transitivity, which itself tends to be higher for ties with positive valence. Hence, closure and strong ties tend to go hand in hand. Further, if closure among the neighbors of a focal actor (say, A) is zero, then A is the unique bridge among all his alters and is said to span a "structural hole" among them (Burt 1992). If closure is not zero, A may still act as a unique bridge for at least some of his alters. (Note that "unique" applies only to the set comprised of A and his alters: closure or local clustering ignores all other actors in the overall network with whom A is not connected, who may very well be connected to one or more of A's alters.)

Centrality and Centralization

Having considered a number of structural properties of networks, we now turn to an important structural property of individual actors within a network: their centrality. We also discuss briefly the extent to which the network is organized around central actors, a characteristic referred to as centralization.

Centrality Centrality describes an actor's importance in the overall network. Once we broaden our perspective beyond a single dyad, some actors will almost certainly be more important or prominent than others in the network. Two questions emerge: How does one define "importance" and, second, how does one identify those actors with an important position in the network? Network analysts have developed several measures of centrality, and have also documented how they pertain to several kinds of "importance." We limit our review to the most popular, which have been implemented in easy-to-use software programs, like Ucinet and NetMiner (Huisman and van Duijn 2005).

Degree centrality The most straightforward measure of centrality consists of simply counting the number of ties, or *degree*, an actor has. If the relationship is not symmetric, it is informative to separate ties sent from ties received (e.g., providing versus receiving advice). The number of ties sent by an actor make up his or her *out-degree* whereas that of ties received make up his or her *in-degree*. In-degree and out-degree indicate different, and often opposite, characteristics. Someone receiving requests for advice from many people is probably viewed as an expert or a thought leader, whereas sending out such a request to many people may indicate a lack of expertise and confidence.

   Although degree centrality in general, and in-degree centrality in particular, is often interpreted as one's "popularity" as a friend, advisor, or alliance partner, it can also be interpreted as a measure of promiscuity.

Closeness centrality Degree centrality considers only the number of actors a focal actor is directly connected to. But what if one is interested in an actor's ability to quickly access information from all over the network, rather than simply from his or her direct social vicinity? Closeness centrality describes how close an actor is to each of the other actors in the entire network. To develop an operational measure, analysts use the concept of *geodesic* or *shortest path* (also known as "degrees of separation"): What is the minimum number of steps through which node A can reach node B? If actors A and B are directly connected, the shortest path will be 1. If they are not directly connected, but share a common contact, it will be 2. If they are connected only through a friend of a friend, the shortest path will be 3, and so on. By computing the shortest path from A to each other actor in the network, we can compute A's average geodesic, or closeness centrality. We can repeat the exercise for any other actor. Note that closeness centrality focuses on *reach* and *reachability* rather than popularity, and is therefore more relevant than degree centrality when one is interested in actors' ability to get or spread information across a network (e.g., marketers trying to identify target customers in a viral campaign).

Betweenness centrality Another facet of centrality captures to what extent an actor is "in the middle" of things. Is the actor a critical intermediary (go-between or bridge) to many other members of the network? Here again, the operational measure uses the idea of geodesic or shortest path. To measure the betweenness centrality of an actor, let's call him Frank, in a given network, one identifies the shortest path between any pair of nodes in that network. If Frank is on that path, he receives one point; if he isn't, he receives zero points. One repeats that procedure for every possible pair of nodes in the network not including Frank, and adds up all his points for his betweenness centrality score. One can repeat this exercise for all other actors in the network, and compute a betweenness centrality score for each.

Betweenness centrality can be quite important in networks in which something flows between nodes (information, goods, money). Being involved in many flows allows an actor to keep abreast of new developments. Further, if an actor is critical to the efficient flow of information, money, and other resources between many pairs of actors, he or she may have control over that flow (distorting information, for example) or may be able to earn a nice "rent" in terms of money or prestige. Thus, betweenness centrality can be a measure of both *information access* and of structural *influence* or *power* in the network.

Other centrality metrics Degree, closeness, and betweenness centrality are the most popular measures, but other centrality metrics may be preferable in specific cases. For instance, *information centrality* generalizes betweenness centrality by considering all paths between any two actors, not only the shortest one. This refinement matters when some actors have a larger degree than others: someone with a high degree is, simply by chance, more likely to be on a shortest path, and one may want to purify one's measure of this artifact. Also, information centrality is more likely to capture the impact of peripheral actors, who can have significant effects on knowledge and disease transmission in a network. Another metric is *eigenvector centrality*, which is the basic idea behind Google's PageRank algorithm (Brin and Page 1998). The name sounds daunting, but the idea is intuitively quite appealing: an actor with high prestige is one who is connected to other actors with high prestige.[12]

Centralization Centrality captures the importance or prominence of the actors in the network. Centralization, in contrast, captures the extent to which the network has a centralized structure, i.e., the extent to which the network is organized around particular focal (central) actors. Several centralization metrics exist, corresponding to different centrality metrics. The general idea is to look for differences between the centrality scores of the most central actor and those of all other actors. Depending on which centrality measures one uses, one obtains different centralization metrics, like degree centralization, closeness centralization, and betweenness centralization.

Subgroups within a Network

Just as marketers are interested in identifying market segments within large groups of customers, social network analysts are interested in identifying subgroups within networks. For example, in the spread of information or the diffusion of products, it is important to localize cohesive subgroups in which diffusion is likely to go faster than average. Just as with market segmentation, a key question is: On what basis should one group actors in a network subgroup? There are three broad approaches in social network analysis: relational or social cohesion, structural equivalence, and structural isomorphism.

Social Cohesion The social cohesion approach identifies densely interconnected regions in the network in which most or all actors are directly tied to one another. Nodes in these dense subgroups tend to not only be directly connected but also share a number of common neighbors. Such redundancy can be important in the diffusion of information, attitudes, and values (Rogers and Kincaid 1981; White and Harary 2001). Moreover, it can enhance stability as the presence of common neighbors makes it harder to sever a tie (Feld 1997). These socially cohesive subgroups are sometimes called *social circles* (e.g., Alba and Kadushin 1976; Granovetter 1982), although sometimes this term is used only if the subgroup in question is informal rather than formal and its members share common interests (Kadushin 1966).

Cohesive subgroups can be identified in several ways. One approach represents the network as a rectangular array or matrix where each row and each column represents a node or actor, and the $(i,j)^{th}$ cell represents the tie from node i to j. For instance, if person i asks person j for advice, then we enter the value 1, otherwise we enter the value 0. We can also use more fine-grained values to represent the strength of the ties. This matrix of direct ties is called the *adjacency matrix* of the network, since it indicates who is a direct social "neighbor" of whom. See Figure 3. The matrix is then analyzed using techniques quite common in market research, such as multidimensional scaling (MDS) and cluster analysis, to reveal subsets of densely interconnected actors.

Another approach divides the entire network into successively smaller subgroups by severing the ties that, if removed, would disconnect a subgroup from the entire network. Unsurprisingly, one can identify these ties as those with the highest betweenness centrality (e.g., Girvan and Newman 2002; Moody and White 2003) or information centrality (Fortunato, Latora, and Marchiori 2004).

A third approach is to zoom in on each node and assess with what other nodes it forms densely interconnected subgroups. In graph theory, the branch of mathematics underlying much of network analysis, the most elementary subgroup is called the *clique*. A clique is a subgroup of at least three actors who are all connected with one another and who is not contained in another clique. (Note that this technical definition is more restrictive than the common-parlance meaning of "clique" as a small but very cohesive set of people but without regard for ties to outsiders.) Because such cliques—where all actors are connected with all other actors—tend to be quite small in size in real-world networks, analysts have also developed a weaker version of the concept called *n*-cliques. In an *n*-clique, all actors are connected by a shortest path of length *n* or less (i.e., either directly or through a maximum of $n - 1$ intermediates), and no other actor in the network has a shortest path distance of *n* or less to each and all members of the *n*-clique. The most popular *n*-clique is the 2-clique where all actors are connected either directly or through one common contact. *N*-cliques come with a number of practical problems. They are sensitive to random error caused by removal of any given node and do not always bring dense interconnectivity to the fore. Further, the number of 2-cliques in even a small network can be large and pairs of 2-cliques can display high levels of overlap, reducing one's ability to identify separate subgroups of practical relevance. Some researchers have therefore followed a two-step approach, where

Figure 3

Sociogram and Adjacency Matrix for a Seven-Actor Network

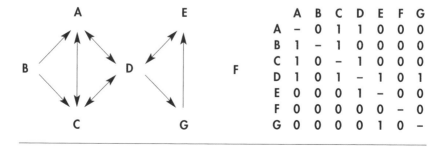

they first identify all the 2-cliques in a network and then perform a cluster analysis based on the overlap between pairs of 2-cliques (e.g., Verbeke and Wuyts 2007). Two other methods of identifying cohesive subgroups may be useful. The first, the k-plex, is based on the notion that such groups should contain actors among whom there are many contacts, but not necessarily perfect connectivity. In a k-plex containing n nodes, all actors are directly connected to at least $n - k$ other members of the k-plex. The k-core is a subgroup in which all actors have direct ties with at least k other actors from the subgroup. Contrary to the k-plex, which is defined on the basis of the maximum number of absent ties from each node to other members, a k-core is defined on the basis of the minimum number of present ties to the members. For example, a subgroup of 10 individuals is a 3-plex if each individual is connected with at least 7 other members. It is a 3-core if all individuals have direct ties with at least 3 other individuals.

The different approaches to identifying cohesive subgroups have complementary strengths and weaknesses. Standard MDS and cluster analysis as well as the newer "edge removal" approach provide a bird's eye view of the network, but additional insight can come from inspecting the k-plexes and k-cores as they provide more information on members of particularly large cohesive subgroups. Thankfully, modern software can list, at the touch of a button, all the subgroups for all values of k for which a k-plex or k-core is defined in a particular network.

The other approaches to identify subgroups do not group together actors who are densely interconnected. Instead, they group together actors whose pattern or portfolio of ties is similar to one another. There are two main approaches to identify actors with such an equivalent position in the network: structural equivalence and structural isomorphism. We discuss both below.

Structural Equivalence *Structural equivalence* refers to the concept of similarity based on common neighbors and common indirect contacts. Thus, it focuses on the overlap of portfolios of contacts between two actors. There are two main approaches to identifying structurally equivalent actors and organizing them into subgroups.

The first approach creates a matrix and then analyzes it using standard techniques common in marketing research. For instance, one may take the adjacency matrix—which represents direct contacts—and transform it into a matrix reflecting similarity in the network's portfolio of ties. One does this by taking each pair of columns i and j in the adjacency matrix, computing a similarity metric between them (e.g., a correlation coefficient or the sum of squared differences), and entering the resulting value into the $(i,j)^{th}$ cell of a new matrix, which one may call a structural equivalence matrix. The matrix can be analyzed using multivariate techniques such as MDS and cluster analysis.

The second approach is called *blockmodeling*. The procedure is implemented in several easy-to-use software packages, and the gist of it is as follows. Take the original adjacency matrix and, if necessary, transform the entries so that they are either 0 or 1. Then, move rows and corresponding columns around so that you obtain 4 submatrices or "blocks" in which the typical value tends to be either 0 or 1. You have now identified two types of positions: actors corresponding to the upper rows and left-hand columns versus those in the lower rows and right-hand columns. You can also collapse the matrix into a 2 × 2 matrix, and round up the average values in each block to either 0 or 1. The resulting "image matrix" gives a bird's eye view of the overall structure of the network. For example, the image matrix of a network of word-of-mouth ties might take the following form:

1 0
1 1

This represents a hierarchical structure in which actors in the top row and actors in the bottom row listen to actors of their own status (upper left and lower right blocks), and where actors in the bottom row listen to actors in the top row (bottom left block) but not vice versa (upper right block). This structure suggests that, in this network, the actors in the top row have a higher status than those in the bottom row. The structure is quite interesting for new product marketing, since it is consistent with the existence of opinion leaders and also captures the "chasm" that has been found to exist between early and late adoption (Van den Bulte and Joshi 2007). Of course, it is quite possible that there are more than two positional groups in the network. One can investigate this by repeating the same procedure for each submatrix. This will produce a larger set of blocks.

Careful analysts will want to explore and investigate structural equivalence using different methods, to avoid falling foul of some idiosyncrasy in the data or analysis. Fortunately, the two different approaches discussed here often yield similar subgroups.

Structural Isomorphism Structural equivalence is a very useful notion, especially if one is interested in competition. Suppliers of similar goods will be competing more intensely with each other when they have high overlap in their customer portfolios. Similarly, five product managers who tend to seek advice or other inputs from the same set of actors (a common superior, engineers in the R&D department, researchers in the analytics group, etc.) will compete with each other for their attention, time, and benevolence. Yet, structural equivalence is not without problems if one is interested in how actors' position in the network is associated with, or even induces, expectations about their behavior.[13] For example, nurses in a hospital may be structurally equivalent if their social connections pertain to the same physicians, administrators, and patients. In this case, structural equivalence will reflect how such nurses will compete for the respect of these physicians, administrators, and patients, and how, in turn, those three sets of actors will compete for these nurses' time and commitment. However, structural equivalence will not reflect the idea that nurses in general are subject to particular expectations given the pattern of their relations to patients, physicians, and administrators in general. This similarity in expectations is better reflected in the concept of *structural isomorphism* (Borgatti and Everett 1992), which focuses on the similarity in the portfolio of ties that need not necessarily involve the same set of third parties. A medical sales rep knowing these general expectations can use them to his benefit and boost prescriptions in different hospitals. He may even transfer that skill to other markets where similar patterns of positions occur. One example is cutting-edge IT products where senior managers make the decision to adopt (physicians), and the users (patients) count on the IT department and tech support staff (nurses) to help them function properly.

Structural equivalence, while usefully highlighting sets of competitors, may also be limiting in business-to-business networks. For instance, firms brokering deals between otherwise disconnected actors may be subject to common informal norms and performance expectations. Even if they work with nonoverlapping sets of buyers and sellers, their business practices may be benchmarked against each other.

So, when one is interested in how network positions are associated with role expectations rather than with competition, the concept of structural isomorphism, which does not require overlap in neighbors but still regards actors as similar if they are connected in the same way to similarly positioned actors, is more useful than the concept of structural equivalence. While structural equivalence reflects "local" similarity of position, structural isomorphism takes a "global" view of the network when identifying similarly positioned actors. Several methods have been developed to achieve this; one of them, called *regular equivalence*, has been implemented in several user-friendly software packages.

Two Puzzles

We conclude our conceptual toolkit with two puzzles that reveal some unexpected consequences of the fundamental characteristics of human networks, especially homophily and transitivity.

Cross-cutting Social Circles Social networks tend to exhibit homophily and transitivity: people tend to connect with others like them and to others with whom they already share an alter, i.e., a common neighbor. Put differently, people tend to sort themselves out into densely interconnected subgroups (because of transitivity) consisting of similar people (homophily). The result can be strong patterns of racial, gender, political, and religious segregation in society, and the presence of many different sub-networks of interest that do not communicate and hence do not share new ideas and practices. Thus, it is commonly believed that homophily is bad for social integration and information flow. That thinking, however, is incomplete: homophily can foster rather than impede integration. Actors can exhibit strong homophily and still tap into many different parts of the network provided that they are homophilous on attributes that are not highly correlated. In fact, being homophilous on attributes that are not highly correlated makes one more likely to connect two different cohesive subgroups or social circles in the network (Blau 1977; Simmel 1955).

As an example, say we are looking at a firm in which employees differ in three socially salient regards: nationality (French versus Hungarian), department (research versus marketing), and being a sports fan (yes versus no). If being French implies being a sports fan and a researcher, and being Hungarian implies not liking sports and being a marketer, then the network of informal communication and friendship will consist of two very homogenous groups between which hardly any interaction takes place. Homophily in departmental affiliation, in nationality, and in leisure interests will mutually reinforce each other. However, if the attributes cross-cut, and being French is not associated with being a sports fan or being a researcher, homophily has a very different effect. A French sports-loving researcher will now have a tendency to seek out marketers (sports-loving and French, but marketers nevertheless). The French sports-loving researcher will also seek out people who prefer other leisure activities to sport (provided they are French and researchers) and Hungarians (provided they are sports fans and researchers). So, homophily will help rather than hurt the flow of information and support *provided* the departments are well mixed with respect to leisure preference and nationality. A second provision must be made: the departments, even when well mixed, must not be so large that, say, a French sports-loving researcher has plenty of fellow French sports-loving researchers to socialize with. Similar effects have been observed in American schools: putting white and black students not just in the same schools but also in the same grades and subject tracks helps the formation of cross-racial friendships, but much less so in very large schools (Moody 2001).

This is an important insight for managers trying to foster more informal social interaction between functional silos, areas of expertise, or communities of practice. By properly managing the makeup of departments, the human tendency to connect with people like oneself can facilitate rather than impede the flow of information and social support across departments.

Small Worlds The expression "it's a small world" is typically uttered when two people who had no previous connection realize they have an acquaintance in common or otherwise trace a social path between them. A related expression is "six degrees of separation," which stems from a famous series of experiments in the 1960s claiming that the shortest path length between two Americans was only about six (on average). In one of those studies Travers and Milgram (1969) gave 296 individuals—196 from Omaha, Nebraska, and 100 from Boston—a small booklet or "passport" and asked them to try and hand or mail that booklet to a stockbroker living in Sharon, Massachusetts, a small town outside Boston, with the constraint that they could pass the booklet only to someone whom they knew on a first-name basis and whom they believed might know the stockbroker or might know somebody who did. Those who received the booklet were given the same instructions, and the process was repeated until the booklet reached the stockbroker. The number of intermediate steps used to reach him varied from 1 to 11, with a median of 5.2. A shortest path with five intervening points counts six links, hence the expression "six degrees of separation." It is important to note—although typically forgotten—that of the 296 possible chains, only 64 or 29% actually arrived. The remaining 232 just petered out, suggesting that the actual distance might be longer, though a correction for this noncompletion rate only raises the number from six to eight (White 1970).[14]

A later study by Korte and Milgram (1970) reports that the number of completed chains was 2½ times as great when both the initial source and the target were both white than when the source was white but the target black. Even so, the mean number of intermediaries on completed chains was again about five to six, and this remained constant over differences in the race of the target person.

It is truly puzzling that such short paths can exist. If, as many studies report, high levels of transitivity, structural balance, and local clustering in human relationships lead to dense clusters where many contacts are "redundant" from an information transfer point of view, how can we observe such small average paths connecting any two points in the network?

The answer came in an important study by Watts and Strogatz (1998) which shows that only small random deviations from transitivity or local clustering are sufficient to create a "small world" where any node can connect with any other node in a few steps. The three networks they investigate (Hollywood actors, the power grid of the western U.S., and the neural network of the worm *Caenorhabditis elegans*) all exhibited this combination of short path length with high local clustering. Several other studies find the same "small world" or "high-local-clustering-yet-short-average-geodesic" pattern in human and organizational networks (e.g., Baum, Shipilov, and Rowley 2003; Davis, Yoo, and Baker 2003; Kogut and Walker 2001; Newman 2001; Powell et al. 2005; Uzzi and Spiro 2005).

This is another important insight for managers trying to enhance the flow of ideas into and within their organization: Local clustering or closure need not rule out the possibility that there are also short paths to other parts of the network. This insight is directly relevant to the next chapter, which addresses social capital: the benefits that actors can derive from specific types of ties and positions.

3
Social Capital

Marketing practitioners are concerned mostly with the consequences of social networks. How and when do network patterns matter? How does network structure affect behaviors as well as the performance of actors both inside and outside the firm? What kinds of social networks are relevant for which types of marketing decisions? The previous chapter provides some concepts to describe networks and the position of actors within them, and hence allows one to frame these questions more precisely. In this chapter, we present a general discussion of the benefits that social networks can provide, a topic which generally goes under the label "social capital."

The core idea of social capital is simply that some networks and network positions confer more advantages to actors than other. Many people use the term but often mean quite different things by it. Social philosophers and political scientists use "social capital" to refer to the norms of reciprocity and trustworthiness that arise from social networks (e.g., Putnam 2000) or simply the informal norms that promote cooperation (e.g., Fukuyama 1995). Such discussions take a macro-level perspective in which the community or even the country, rather than the firm or the customer, serves as the unit of analysis. Also, social networks are seen in terms of civic engagement, i.e., the involvement of people in their community, and the actual structure of the network is ignored.

An alternate conception of social networks—and one that is more useful to marketers—has been developed by sociologists. They focus on individual actors (micro-level) and on the salient network features providing advantages. Actor-level social capital is traditionally defined broadly as those aspects of social structure that can be used by actors to realize their interests (Coleman 1990) or as the ability of actors to secure benefits by virtue of membership in social networks or other social structures (Portes 1998).[15] These benefits include (1) access to information and other resources, (2) improved coordination through higher trust, (3) control over the flow of information and resources which allows one to appropriate value, and (4) status which allows one to appropriate value (Burt 1992; Lin 2001; Portes 1998).

How do social networks provide such benefits? Theory and research point to the resources of one's direct contacts (e.g., Lin 2001), the number of ties (e.g., Ball et al. 2001), the strength of ties (e.g., Krackhardt 1992), closure or local clustering (e.g., Coleman 1988, 1990; Granovetter 1992), and "bridging structural holes" (e.g., Burt 1992) as the relevant features. We elaborate on each below.

Resources of Direct Contacts

Level of Resources The more resources are at the disposal of an actor's direct contacts or network neighbors, the more likely it is that the actor will be able to access some resources to his or her benefit. For a solution to a problem, one is better off asking an expert, or at least someone with experience, than a novice. If one is looking to raise money, one is better off having wealthy relatives and friends than poor ones. As folk wisdom says, it's not what you know but who you know that matters. Less obvious is that the diversity of resources is also important.

Diversity of Resources People and firms have a variety of needs that require a variety of resources to address them. For example, to avoid being stuck on a single technological trajectory, firms must maintain ties with other firms and institutions working on a variety of technologies. Even the narrowly defined resource of social support from neighbors, friends, and relatives may include information, material aid (money, goods, and services), emotional aid, and companionship. It is unlikely that one will get all these four types of resources from the same person. While parents and adult children provide a broad spectrum of aid, neighbors and other frequently seen alters are more likely to provide material aid, and women are more likely to provide emotional support than men (Walker, Wasserman, and Wellman 1994).

From a network point of view, access to a diversity of resources typically requires that one is connected to a diversity of actors, in other words, that one is positioned at the intersection of several social circles rather than only within a single cohesive subgroup. Such positions also tend to be associated with high closeness and betweenness centrality; simply having many ties (degree centrality) is not enough.

Alters' Social Capital Alters' resources not only may consist of financial capital, physical capital (e.g., raw materials), and human capital (e.g., knowledge) but may also include the alters' social capital (e.g., access to a decision maker). Thus, the value of alters lies in the resources they control directly and in the indirect access they provide to other resources. An actor can benefit from alters' resources through direct leverage and through indirect "two-step leverage" (Boissevain 1974; Gargiulo 1993) or "structural leverage" (Krackhardt 1996).

Number of Ties

Having more ties allows an actor to put smaller demands on each alter, and provides redundancy or slack which is useful in case some alters are not able or willing to provide assistance. In addition, empirical evidence indicates that, when quality is uncertain, buyers use a vendor's number of ties (or degree) as an indicator of that vendor's status and quality, which allows the vendor to appropriate value through higher sales or higher prices (Ball et al. 2001).

Strength of Ties

Strong ties are more valuable than weak ties, keeping everything else constant. High-frequency ties increase the opportunities one has to communicate one's needs and to assess others' available resources. High frequency is particularly useful when resource transfers are complex and require a lot of tailoring or back-and-forth coordination, as in the deployment of a CRM system. High frequency combined with long duration may also be associated with the presence of a shared language and a deep knowledge of each other's routines, which can further boost the ability to transfer complex knowledge and provide complex support services. Actors with whom one has high-valence ties will be more benevolent and hence more willing to provide support. Finally, long-standing ties may boost willingness to provide resources as the cumulative number of past interactions—i.e., frequency multiplied by duration—is likely to increase alters' confidence in reciprocation (assuming that the actor requesting support has indeed reciprocated on previous occasions).

Multiplexity, the presence of multiple kinds of ties with the same alter, will also contribute to the strength of the "total" tie, by providing more opportunities to assess the alters' ability to provide support, more opportunities to request support, and more ways to build positive valence. In addition, multiplexity increases the number of ways in which any favor can be reciprocated in the future—advice, for example, can be repaid by respect or a commercial transaction.

Overall, tie strength provides two kinds of benefits. First, it improves access to alters' resources through a triple route of opportunity, ability, and motivation. Second, it helps the coordination of activities between two parties through richer information transfer and through higher expectations that acts of cooperation will be reciprocated.

It is important to note here that the long-term nature of ties has, in and of itself, only limited power to activate support. As discussed above, what matters is the ability, opportunity, and motivation to share resources. Further, the aspects of tie strength we discuss here map relatively well into the large literature on trust in marketing, where trust is defined as an attribution of ability (i.e., presence of resources and ability to transfer), honesty (intention to honor an implicit or explicit promise of reciprocation), and benevolence (willingness to support even without expectation of reciprocation). Similarly, high interaction frequency enhances the ability to transfer resources; tie frequency and duration provide experience with the alter and hence information about likely intentions and future behavior; and positive tie valence, finally, increases the motivation to treat the other benevolently, or at least not malevolently.

Closure and Local Clustering

Having a densely knit network makes it easier to mobilize support and resources because the presence of common third parties supports the emergence and enforcement of norms of cooperation (e.g., Greif 1993). In a densely knit network, an actor whose request for help is denied can damage the refuser's reputation by bad-mouthing him or her among their common contacts. Conversely, if the request is honored, the actor can boost the helper's reputation. Network density is also thought to foster identification with the group, further facilitating cooperation (Portes and Sensenbrenner 1993). Hence, actors with a densely knit network may be better able to motivate their contacts to make their resources available when called upon.

Closure may also affect the ability to transfer resources. Specifically, greater social closure may lead to greater cognitive cohesion characterized by shared language, codes, and stories among the members of a subgroup, which in turn can boost the ability to transfer resources, especially complex knowledge (Nahapiet and Ghoshal 1998).

Strong ties tend to be associated with closure (via transitivity), and both strong ties and closure facilitate trust and cooperation through benevolence. As a result, one may have the impression that the benefits of strong ties ("relational embeddedness") and of closure ("structural embeddedness") go hand in hand and are generated in the same fashion. That is not quite true. Tie strength is associated with particularistic or particularized trust: the trustor expects the trustee to reciprocate based on prior experience, positive valence, and possibly also multiplexity of their dyadic tie. Closure, in contrast, is associated with generalized and enforceable trust: the trustor expects the trustee to reciprocate because of the penalties enforced by common alters in case of nonreciprocation and other malfeasance. Note the differences in who is being trusted and in the causal mechanism. Closure leads to *cooperative expectation based on enforcement mechanisms* that are effective only in closed network structures but do not require any prior history or positive affect between the two parties for cooperation to emerge. In contrast, strong ties lead to *cooperative expectation based on the greater ability, opportunity, and motivation* to cooperate that stem from experience and affect within the dyad, independently of the larger structure in which the tie is embedded.

Whereas tie strength facilitates the motivation, ability, and opportunities to transfer resources, closure enhances the motivation and ability, but not the opportunities, to do so. In fact, as we discuss next, network closure actually reduces the opportunities to locate valuable resources.

Bridge Positions Spanning Structural Holes

Network closure leads to high redundancy among an actor's alters: when everyone is connected to everyone, no one has unique information. So closure does not provide any actor with an information advantage but keeps everyone at parity. In general, the extent to which an actor has an information advantage depends on the extent to which he or she spans structural holes, that is, uniquely links separate parts of the network (Burt 1992). Being connected to many poorly interconnected actors offers important *information benefits:* one gets more varied bits of information and one gets each bit sooner than the average network member. In addition, spanning structural holes provides the actor with multiple interpretations of the same events, permitting cross-validation of information and more reliable knowledge (Burt 1999).

Spanning a structural hole also provides an actor with *control benefits:* an actor spanning a structural hole in the network, through his or her control of the flow of information and other resources, also controls joint projects between these otherwise unconnected parts of the network. Such a brokerage position creates opportunities for arbitrage and rent extraction (Burt 1992). Within firms, managers controlling joint projects in this manner can gain visibility and faster promotion. In commercial transactions, firms able to bring together otherwise unconnected actors and resources can earn a supra-normal profit. The simplest example is that of a broker with a monopoly in bringing together demand and supply. The idea also applies to new business venturing. The so-called Austrian school of economics considers bringing together otherwise disconnected ideas and resources into value-creating projects as the essence of entrepreneurship (Kirzner 1973, 1979).

Because structural holes can be defined locally or globally, theoretical statements and empirical studies about them sometimes conflict. In the local definition, a focal actor is said to span a hole when any of his or her direct neighbors are not connected through a direct tie. In the global definition, a focal actor is said to span a hole when any of his or her direct neighbors are not connected through a direct tie or even an indirect tie involving nodes unconnected to the focal actor. In other words, the local definition looks only at the focal actor's ego-network, whereas the global one takes into account the entire network. The global definition is the theoretically more rigorous one, but many studies using only ego-network data use the local definition. Also, the local definition has some substantive advantage: if two neighbors of A are connected only through A and through another path involving five intermediaries, then those two neighbors are not very likely to use the long path successfully and A is very likely to indeed have information and control benefits.

In conclusion, having a portfolio of nonoverlapping ties and a bridge position provides an actor with access to unique information and with control or brokerage opportunities. Simmel (1950) referred to this idea as the principle of *tertius gaudens*, the third who benefits or enjoys. Note, the rationale here is quite opposite to that of closure: whereas our discussion of closure emphasized value creation through cooperation benefits, the emphasis of the "structural holes" or "tertius gaudens" argument lies on value appropriation through superior information and control.

"The Strength of Weak Ties"

Strong ties have many benefits and hence are a major form of social capital. Yet, "The Strength of Weak Ties" (Granovetter 1973) is one of the most famous theoretical ideas involving social networks. Here, we address the paradox.

Granovetter's insight is based on a study of the social mechanisms through which people find employment. The research setting was Newton, a small suburb of Boston. In 1969, a random sample of 280 professional, technical, and managerial workers filled out a questionnaire, and 100 of them were also interviewed. Granovetter finds that almost 56 percent of the respondents got their jobs through social contacts (which included the employer), compared to only 19 percent through direct "cold call" application and 18 percent through formal means including job ads. But, of the 54 interviewees who found their job through contacts, 16.7 percent reported that they were seeing their contact "often," 55.6 percent "occasionally," and 27.8 percent "rarely" (Granovetter 1995, p. 53). In other words, frequent contacts accounted for a much smaller proportion of jobs taken than less frequent contacts. This was odd, and hence interesting, and Granovetter put forth the following explanation: people we know intimately and see often (strong ties) all tend to know each other well (transitivity). As a consequence, they tend to share the same limited information (closure) and are less able to offer new information on job leads. People we know only casually (weak ties), on the other hand, are less likely to know each other (lower transitivity and closure), and are more likely to have new information on job leads. Hence, Granovetter concludes, weak ties are more valuable than strong ties when it comes to job leads.

It is important to note that Granovetter's argument really is not about the strength of ties but about closure (and the resulting redundancy) and bridging structural holes (and the resulting information advantage). Thus, it is consistent with our discussion of social capital and the benefits of strong ties. As Granovetter wrote several years later: "The argument ... implies that only *bridging* weak ties are of special value to individuals; the significance of weak ties is that they are far more likely to be bridges than strong ties" (1982, p. 112, emphasis in original) and "Weak ties provide people with access to information and resources beyond those available in their own social circles; but strong ties have greater motivation to be of assistance and are typically more available" (p. 113).

To better grasp the mechanism at work, consider a study of social networks in 1988 China (Bian 1997). At that time, good jobs assigned by authorities were scarce and highly coveted. In such a situation, weak ties will not offer much value. First, anyone knowing about a lead might share that valuable information only with those with whom they have a close relationship. Second, closure might be an asset as it would further motivate those with a job lead to share it with you rather than with someone else. In fact, the study's findings contrast starkly with those of Granovetter's study of 1969 Newton, but are very much in line with his arguments about the value of bridging: (1) jobs were acquired through strong ties more frequently than through weak ties, (2) both direct and indirect ties were used to obtain help from job-assigning authorities, (3) job seekers and their ultimate helpers were indirectly connected through intermediaries to whom both were strongly tied, and (4) job seekers using indirect ties were more likely to obtain better jobs than those using direct ties. In short, having ties helped in locating jobs, tie strength and closure helped in getting the job, but jobs obtained through indirect (and presumably bridging) ties—if obtained!—were better.

As we already noted, weak ties suffer from a low-motivation problem. As the China study by Bian (1997) illustrates, weak ties will not lead to an information advantage if that information is closely guarded. In some cases, this low-motivation problem of weak ties diminishes their value even in the search for "cheap" information. A recent study documents this in a rather dramatic way.

Remember that in the original small world experiments most chains did not reach their target. This suggests that most people were either *not able* or *not willing* to make the requested connections, but whether ability or willingness was the bigger culprit is unclear. A recent study was designed along the same lines as the original studies in the 1960s but used a much larger number of starting points (over 24,000), email rather than postal mail, and did not limit itself to the U.S. Participants registered online and were randomly allocated one of 18 target persons from 13 countries, including a professor at an Ivy League university, a veterinarian in the Norwegian Army, an archival inspector in Estonia, a technology consultant in India, and a policeman in Australia. Participants were informed that their task was to "help relay a message to their allocated target by passing the message to a social acquaintance whom they considered 'closer' than themselves to the target" (Dodds, Muhamad, and Watts 2003, p. 827). There was clear evidence of homophily: men passed messages more frequently to men (57%) and women to other women (61%). In addition, people used homophily as a basis to decide whom to forward the email to: the acquaintance's geographical proximity to the target and similarity of occupation were mentioned in over half the cases as a reason for selecting a particular acquaintance to be a recipient. None of this is very surprising. Intriguingly enough, the average length of completed chains was five for chains that started and ended in the same country and seven for others. However, the big surprise was that of the 24,163 chains started, only 384 actually reached their target. In other words, the noncompletion rate was a staggering 98.4%! (So much for the Internet turning the world into a global village.) People were clearly not using their networks effectively. Recipients who did not forward their message after a week were contacted by the researchers and asked why they had not done so. "Less than 0.3% of those contacted claimed that they could not think of an appropriate recipient, suggesting that lack of interest or incentive, not difficulty, was the main reason for chain termination" (Dodds, Muhamad, and Watts 2003, p. 828). While senders may have chosen to rely on recipients who were able to continue the chain, it appears the latter were *not motivated* to do so. Here again, the "motivation deficit" of weak ties is the likely culprit.

As both general theory and the China and Internet studies suggest, social capital is more complex and richer than simply reaching out to one's acquaintances. Using weak ties may improve one's ability to reach farther into the network, but won't necessarily help one to mobilize the actor and his or her resources.

The Dark Side of Social Capital

The social network mechanisms that generate opportunities and benefits can also impose constraints and costs. Here are the main problems (Portes 1998; Portes and Sensenbrenner 1993; Uzzi 1997).

When many actors in a network depend on the resources and loyalty of a few central actors, the network may suffer from lack of robustness. Further, the excessive demands on successful and well-endowed actors, which may take the form of "free riding," will not allow those actors to appropriate the value of their efforts, thus curtailing their motivation and entrepreneurship. Free riding may also erode cooperation and support norms.

While cohesion may foster group identification and trust among members, a cohesive subgroup's relative separation from the rest of the network can also generate distrust of outsiders and stickiness ("hoarding") of information. Newcomers may have restricted access to resources and opportunities. The normative pressures in close-knit social networks can lead to over-emphasis on group sustenance to the detriment of economic efficiency and result in restrictions on the autonomy, individuality, and creativity of members.

The advantages offered to those spanning structural holes represent mostly a win-lose value appropriation situation: one actor's gain typically comes at the expense of another. Excessive jockeying for position by actors trying to win an information or a control advantage can even hurt overall network performance.

4

Networks among Customers

In this chapter, we use theory and empirical evidence to critically frame the effect of inter-customer networks on customer behavior. Most evidence comes from the realm of new product diffusion, i.e., how new products get adopted and gain market acceptance. There is less evidence about the effects of social networks on preference for and purchase of existing products. As to the connection between social network structure and cognitive structures (relevant for understanding brand equity and brand communities), we are not aware of any rigorous quantitative evidence. We discuss each of these areas in turn.

Our review of the relevant knowledge on customer networks does not provide a ringing endorsement of "viral marketing" and similar practices. Instead, we identify several social network issues that managers must think about and we provide some critical assessment of what can be taken for granted or not. We first discuss the area of new product diffusion. We next turn to existing brands, and conclude with a brief discussion of transactions among customers.

Social Contagion and New Products

Researchers from various disciplines have long studied how innovations diffuse through populations of individuals, households, and organizations. Sociologists have offered the important insight that innovation diffusion may be driven by social contagion, i.e., actors' adoption behavior is a function of their exposure to other actors' knowledge, attitude, or behavior concerning the innovation. This raises several issues: Why does such contagion occur? How prevalent is it? How does network structure affect that process? How can marketers take advantage of contagion?

Why Does Contagion Occur? Different theories of social contagion describe different causal mechanisms for social influence. These apply to both consumer and business markets.

Awareness and interest The social influence process may simply consist of the spread of awareness about a new product. This may occur via previous adopters who talk about the new product with others who have not adopted yet. However, the sources of contagion need not have adopted the product; they may simply be aware of it and have sufficiently strong feelings to discuss the product. Further, the transfer of information need not be "active" as in a conversation or email. People may simply observe a new product—houses with satellite dishes or people with iPods, for example—and that observation may interest them sufficiently that they will seek information about it.

Marketers should not take for granted that adopters become aware through contagion. Word-of-mouth among confidants is not likely to drive awareness for products that are easy to observe in daily life or that are much talked about or advertised in the media, whereas the opposite is true for products that are illegal or otherwise taboo in mainstream media (e.g., Lee 1969). In fact, the new product diffusion literature finds, overall, that personal channels (including word-of-mouth) are less important than impersonal channels (commercial or not) in creating awareness (Rogers 2003).

Belief updating People may update their beliefs about the costs and benefits of adopting the new product after discussing it with previous adopters or after observing the outcomes of adoption (e.g., a schoolmate's increased status on the playground). This additional information may affect beliefs in several ways. First, actors may revise their beliefs about how well the product performs on particular attributes or dimensions ("Hmm, it's clear from what Bob told and showed me that those MP3 players are easier to use than I thought"). Second, even if the new information does not lead to an upward or downward revision of beliefs, it may confirm current beliefs, thus reducing uncertainty about the product. Different disciplines focus on slightly different facets of this process, but all agree on the basic idea of belief updating through social contagion (also called social learning). Examples are Bayesian updating through social learning under risk aversion in economics and decision science (e.g., Chatterjee and Eliashberg 1990; Roberts and Urban 1988), vicarious learning and modeling in social psychology (e.g., Bandura 1986), and mimesis in sociology (e.g., DiMaggio and Powell 1983).

Belief updating through social contagion is particularly important to adoption in certain situations. The first are situations where potential adopters view the product as complex with difficult-to-understand links between features and benefits. Note here that perceived complexity is a function both of the actual product and of actors' experience and self-confidence. The second are situations where commercial communication channels have little source credibility—an issue nowadays among teenagers and health care providers. The third type of situation where belief updating through contagion is likely to be important are cases where the product's performance or utility varies across actors, so the potential adopters want to know not simply whether the product is "good in general" but "good for folks like us." Here feedback from actors like oneself can be critical. B2B marketers have long capitalized on references from satisfied customers to get additional sales. These references need not come from prestigious firms or national thought leaders. In fact, potential adopters are likely to find firms that are similar to them to be a more relevant source of information. Similarly, individual consumers may want to know what other people like themselves—rather than some expert in a white lab coat—think about the product.

Normative pressure Social influence may occur through normative pressures, as when actors experience discomfort when peers whose approval they value have adopted an innovation but they have not (e.g., Coleman, Katz, and Menzel 1966; Davis, Bagozzi, and Warshaw 1989; DiMaggio and Powell 1983). The so-called "theory of reasoned action," developed in the 1970s, considers product beliefs and normative compliance to be the two determinants of attitude toward the product and the brand. However, the idea that social influence can operate via both informational and normative routes is quite old (e.g., Deutsch and Gerard 1955).

The importance of normative contagion varies across customers. For instance, countries with a national culture exhibiting higher levels of collectivism or higher respect for power and authority tend to show patterns of new product diffusion that are more consistent with social contagion than other countries (Van den Bulte and Stremersch 2004). There are also differences between consumers from the same country in how sensitive they are to normative pressure, as we discuss below.

The importance of normative contagion may also vary across products. Specifically, the extent to which a new product conforms to existing norms can affect the extent to which social acceptance by others affects one's own adoption (Rogers 2003). The adoption of contraceptives is a classic example.

Competitive concerns Social contagion may also be driven by the concern that one's rivals who have adopted the innovation might gain a competitive edge unless one adopts as well. This is likely to be an important driver of contagion among competing firms (e.g., Hannan and McDowell 1987), but may also operate among individuals concerned about their status in their community and networks (Burt 1987).

The fierceness with which firms compete against each other, the extent to which they all use the same technologies, processes, and business models, and the extent to which the new product or technology is likely to contribute to profitability or competitive advantage are likely to affect how much contagion through competitive pressure occurs (e.g., Mansfield 1961). Competitive pressure may operate similarly in consumer markets: products that clearly signal one's consumer identity and status may be more subject to social contagion than other products.

Complementary network effects As discussed earlier, such network effects occur when the benefits of use, and hence of adoption, increase with the number of prior adoptions. This effect may be direct, as with point-to-point communication devices like telephones and fax machines, or indirect, operating through the increased supply of complementary products, as with videocassette recorders and pre-recorded tapes (Katz and Shapiro 1994), or through the increased supply of supporting infrastructure such as video rental stores (Brown 1981; Delacroix and Rao 1994).[16]

As mentioned in Chapter 1, complementarity issues are typically more pronounced in product categories with competing technological standards. Van den Bulte and Stremersch (2004) find that product categories with competing standards exhibit patterns of new product diffusion that are more consistent with social contagion than other products do.

How Prevalent Is Social Contagion? Since the role of social contagion in driving new product diffusion is likely to depend on product and market characteristics, it is difficult to measure its "general" prevalence. Further, what appears to be social contagion can sometimes be a reflection of other dynamics. Classic studies by Katz and Lazarsfeld (1955) and Coleman, Katz, and Menzel (1966), for instance, document that awareness of and attitudes toward new products can be affected by mass media exposure and companies' marketing efforts, as well as by social contagion. More recent research shows that bell-shaped adoption curves—often interpreted as evidence of social contagion—can also result from population heterogeneity (Bemmaor 1994; Bonus 1973; Thirtle and Ruttan 1987). For instance, when a product's price decreases at a constant percentage rate over time—possibly because of experience curve effects, a price-skimming strategy, or simply commoditization—and the maximum price that people or households are willing to pay is lognormally distributed—for instance, because it is a fixed proportion of household income which itself is (roughly) lognormally distributed—then the resulting curve graphing the number of adoptions over time will be mathematically identical to a smooth bell curve following the so-called normal distribution. The argument for caution is not purely mathematical but also empirical. In a re-analysis of a major study in sociology (Coleman, Katz, and Menzel 1966) that is often credited for documenting that innovation diffusion is driven by social contagion (Rogers 2003), Van den Bulte and Lilien (2001) find that all evidence of social contagion disappears once they control for advertising. While they cautiously note that this did not mean that contagion was not truly at work, their re-analysis does indicate that skepticism is appropriate.

Overall, these results indicate that the positive relationship between the prevalence of prior adoption among one's network alters and the likelihood of one's own adoption—typically interpreted as evidence of social contagion—may stem, at least in part, from other factors that change over time but that are excluded from the model. This is hardly a novel insight, but it is often ignored by marketing practitioners and academics. Granovetter (1978) cites the case where individuals appear to react to one another but actually respond to a common, external influence. He offers this quote from Weber ([1921] 1968): "Thus, if at the beginning of a shower a number of people on the street put up their umbrellas at the same time, this would not ordinarily be a case of action mutually oriented to that of each other, but rather of all reacting in the same way to the like need of protection from the rain" (p. 23).

How Does Social Network Structure Affect Contagion? Mindful of the caveats noted above, a manager may want to better understand how network structure affects new product adoption and how to exploit that structure to his or her advantage. We approach the issue, first, from a macro and abstract perspective, in which we review some results on how the overall network structure affects the extent and speed of diffusion. Then, from a micro and substantive perspective, we raise three issues that managers must confront before engaging in a campaign that targets any special nodes in the network.

Macro-level perspective Obviously, a disease, a bit of gossip, or a new product will spread more rapidly over a highly dense network where any node can be reached from any other node in only one or two steps. Conversely, when all nodes are disconnected, they cannot contaminate each other. But what if, say, there is a network of 10,000 nodes where each has only 20 ties to other nodes? How will tie structure affect how far and how fast the disease (or bit of gossip, product, etc.) spreads? Especially, will transitivity and local clustering facilitate or impede diffusion?

Some mathematical models show that as transitivity increases, a disease is less likely to spread throughout a population (e.g., Frenzen and Nakamoto 1993; Keeling 1999; Newman 2003). That makes perfect sense: in a population with high transitivity (and hence local clustering), a disease will tend to reach individuals who already have the disease. Thus the rate at which the disease infects new victims is lower than if all the individuals it reached were susceptible. Note that the mechanism and logic at work here are identical to those underlying the strength-of-weak-ties argument. By the same logic, one would expect that higher clustering leads to slower diffusion of the disease, in addition to a lower ceiling on the total number of nodes infected. This has been confirmed in some studies (e.g., Frenzen and Nakamoto 1993).

However, if there are enough intransitive bridging ties such that every subgroup is at least indirectly connected with every other subgroup, then the high transitivity and density within those subgroups will help rather than impede the spread of the disease (Frenzen and Nakamoto 1993; Ball, Mollison, and Scalia-Tomba 1997; Newman 2003). The reason is simply that the disease will spread more rapidly *within* the subgroups the denser they are and that the bridging ties between the subgroups ensure that the disease continues to spread *between* subgroups as well. In sum, transitivity and local density always help the disease to spread locally, but it helps the disease to spread globally as well only if the transitivity is not so high that it comes at the expense of bridging ties among the dense subgroups or communities.

Differences in people's susceptibility to the disease can also play a critical role in how far a disease will spread. When people have a low resistance or threshold to the disease, they will get infected as soon as they get in touch with the pathogen. One contact with another infected person may be enough. When people have a high resistance or threshold to the disease, their chance of getting infected after one or two contacts may be low. However, even high resistance will break down after repeated exposure—and repeated exposure is much more likely in a densely clustered subset of actors. So, while low clustering helps spread the disease among people with a low threshold, high clustering helps contaminate people with a high threshold (Watts 2002).

This insight has important implications for new product diffusion and viral marketing. When all consumers have low acceptance or adoption thresholds, local clustering is bad for marketing efforts. This is the most obvious scenario (e.g., Üstüner and Godes 2006). But when consumers have various acceptance or adoption thresholds, a mixture of dense clusters interconnected by some bridging ties is optimal: local clustering will "wear out" the highly resistant customers, while the bridges will help spread the disease among the clusters (provided that the nodes linking the clusters to each other have very low thresholds so that the disease can gain a foothold in a previously untouched cluster simply by one contact with an infected node from a different cluster).

To exploit this insight, one must translate the concept of "threshold" to the marketing context. Most models of persuasion or adoption suggest a multi-step process. The best-known sequence may be Awareness-Interest-Desire-Action (AIDA), but there are many others. Rogers (2003) has suggested five product characteristics associated with diffusion speed that can be interpreted as five different dimensions in which hurdles or thresholds can be high or low: (1) relative advantage over existing products and solutions, (2) compatibility with current norms and beliefs, (3) complexity, (4) observability of earlier adopters and their outcomes, and (5) ease of trial without making a major commitment of resources.

Let's now apply those basic frameworks to a marketing context. To spread awareness of a brand or company name, one has to overcome an attention hurdle, but nothing else. Similarly, a product that is cheap but provides major benefits to the customer and is low-risk as well will not be associated with high hurdles: such a product will be bought as soon as people are aware of it and the product is phys-ically available. In such cases, a standard media campaign or a straightforward buzz marketing campaign that spreads a simple message and ignores the network struc-ture will be sufficient to create the awareness that is needed to overcome the adop-tion threshold. However, when the message is more complex or induces fears (e.g., convincing women of the benefits of testing for breast cancer) or the product has a high price, unclear benefits, or some risks involved, the adoption threshold will vary across people depending on their income, their experience with similar prod-uct, and their risk aversion. In such cases, simple buzz marketing will not work as people will need to hear a more complex message, and will want input from sever-al other sources, preferably from people they truly trust. Also, in such a scenario, local clustering—which is inefficient for simple innovations with uniformly low adoption thresholds—becomes an asset in the marketing effort.

So, overall network structure can have a large effect on the extent and speed of a diffusion process. From a managerial point of view, however, the important ques-tion is: How can marketers exploit the network to speed up the acceptance of new products?

Micro-level perspective An obvious approach is to identify the best-connected actors and motivate them to talk about the product, so that adoption occurs as quickly as possible. Theory and research suggest, however, some more sophisticat-ed ideas.

The first issue to consider is that imitators need not imitate only those actors they are directly connected to. Direct ties will be important for spreading aware-ness and interest and for belief updating. Normative pressure is more diffuse, but one can still expect that it will be stronger when operating across direct ties. Something similar is likely to hold for complementarity effects: they will be stronger if operating across direct ties (e.g., people will care about the entire installed base for the PlayStation 3, but will be disproportionately affected by friends who have one). For competitive pressure, direct ties simply do not matter. What matters is structural equivalence—overlap in one's portfolio of ties with the portfolio of other actors—not whether one is directly connected to those equiva-lently positioned actors. From a managerial perspective, that means that when competitive pressure is the source of social contagion, the best "seeding points" for marketing are not necessarily the most central actors, i.e., those connected to the most others, but those who are structurally equivalent to the most others.

The second issue to consider is which tie is most relevant for which social con-tagion driver, whether conformity to norms, risk aversion, or other. Friendship, kin, and perhaps mentoring at work are likely to be the relevant ties for normative issues, whereas asking for technical guidance is more likely to be the relevant tie for risk reduction.

The third issue is the overall network density and structure. If the network is rather dense, then anything traveling over the network can do so quite rapidly, and strategically selecting special nodes as "seeding points" will hardly affect the speed of diffusion. If the network consists of disconnected cohesive groups, then one needs to target at least one actor in each group to serve as a seeding point. Exactly which one need not matter much. If the network is a "small world" of dense subgroups which are loosely interconnected, then the actors bridging the subgroups are more likely to be key. The most realistic case may well be the latter: networks that contain sets of actors with relatively high density among them, but with at least some of them also having quite a few connections to outsiders. In that case, one should consider using a targeting decision rule with two criteria: each seeding point should have relatively many connections, but the seeding points should have only little overlap in their portfolios. The latter will reduce redundancy and hence reduce the number of seeding points one needs to activate or enroll to "cover" most of the network.[17] This idea not only makes sense "on paper"; a controlled field experiment has shown it to be more effective than standard rules to identify seeding points to enroll in a campaign (Valente et al. 2003). This brings us to the next issue: using opinion leaders to leverage one's marketing efforts and speed up product diffusion.

How Can Marketers Take Advantage of Contagion Through Opinion Leaders? As we have discussed, some actors are more influential than others and can serve as important seeding points in the diffusion process. Ideally, these so-called opinion leaders combine four characteristics: (1) being interested in and up to date about new products, (2) being early adopters themselves, (3) having a central location in the network, and (4) engaging in many conversations about new products. Before discussing these characteristics, let us address four popular misconceptions about opinion leadership.

Four misconceptions The first misconception is that there are "generalized" opinion leaders or "influentials" (e.g., Keller and Berry 2003)—although marketers' jobs would be much simplified if there were. There do not appear to be generalized opinion leaders in large communities and modern cities (e.g., Katz and Lazarsfeld 1955; Merton 1949; Myers and Robertson 1972; Silk 1966), and claims to the contrary are inconsistent with the large empirical research on the topic reviewed by Weimann (1994). This is hardly surprising. A person may be a leader in one category or even several related categories (King and Summers 1970), but will not have the expertise or source credibility to act as an information leader across the board. Normative leadership may cut across more categories, but even there the role is not all encompassing. In modern life, people are members of many social groups and have multiple reference groups, and no actors have normative opinion leadership in all realms.

The second misconception, popularized by Gladwell (2000), is that each characteristic of the ideal opinion leader corresponds to a particular type of person (apart from the obvious early adopters, the types he mentions are "mavens" who are up to date, "connectors" who are well connected, and "salesmen" who convincingly get the word out). Turning traits into types is a rhetorical ploy that writers and teachers sometimes turn to, but it is not a sound basis for one's marketing effort in this case, since the presence of one trait does not exclude the presence of another.

The third misconception, less prevalent nowadays, is that opinion leaders must combine all four characteristics. The four characteristics are actually far from perfectly correlated (e.g., Weimann 1994), suggesting that identifying actors as opinion leaders only if they combine all four characteristics is not only a difficult but also a futile task. Worse, it can be dysfunctional, as it would imply ignoring well-connected actors who tend to have a negative assessment of new products and do not endorse or adopt them (e.g., Becker 1970; Leonard-Barton 1985).

The fourth misconception is that one is either an opinion leader or an opinion seeker. This idea may go back to the original two-step flow hypothesis, which states that "ideas often flow *from* radio and print *to* the opinion leaders and *from* them to the less active sections of the population" (Lazarsfeld, Berelson, and Gaudet 1944, p. 151; emphasis in original). While early studies focus on information flows from opinion leaders to opinion seekers, subsequent research documents extensive information exchange among opinion leaders and even from opinion seekers to leaders (e.g., Coulter, Feick, and Price 2002; Katz and Lazarsfeld 1955; Weimann 1994). Researchers also find substantial interaction among opinion seekers themselves.[18] Finally, a study developing scales of opinion leadership and opinion seeking finds the two constructs to be only weakly correlated—and positively rather than negatively (Flynn, Goldsmith, and Eastman 1996). In short, word-of-mouth is typically a two-way process where people often send as well as receive information and opinions from others.

Four characteristics of an ideal opinion leader Let us now return to the four characteristics of an ideal opinion leader and why they matter.

Opinion leaders who are interested in and up to date about new products will be more convincing and hence more able to influence others. They will also seek out new information about products and pay attention to it when provided by a firm. In general, the large body of research on this issue indicates a strong relationship between opinion leadership and product interest and involvement (e.g., Coulter, Feick, and Price 2002; Myers and Robertson 1972). From a marketing point of view, this suggests that the cost to contact leaders may be lower than average. However, since opinion leaders tend to have many demands on their time, this advantage may be diminished (in part because it is "competed away" by marketers of other products).

As early adopters, opinion leaders have direct experience with the product, which increases their source credibility and ability to influence others.[19] It is important to note, however, that opinion leaders are not always early adopters. Baumgarten (1975) finds that slightly less than half of consumers in the top third in opinion leadership are also in the top third in speed of adoption. While opinion leaders did tend to adopt early more often than what one might expect based on chance alone, the overlap between opinion leadership and early adoption was small. Other studies have found similar, weakly positive relations between the two constructs (e.g., Summers 1971). In a very interesting study, Becker (1970) documents an episode in which opinion leaders did not like or endorse an innovation because it conflicted with the source of their power; in this case, actors at the periphery of the network were the first to adopt. Early adoption by peripheral rather than central players has also been observed in business markets. The diffusion of programming formats and business models among radio stations (Leblebici et al. 1991) and the diffusion of digital technologies in the film business (Grover 2006) are two examples. Further, mathematical-theoretical modeling shows that people making up their minds independently (as opinion leaders rather than opinion seekers tend to do) may adopt at any point in time rather than only early on, leading to the somewhat surprising result that the last 30% of adopters may consist not of opinion seekers or followers but of people making up their minds independently (Van den Bulte and Joshi 2007).

Having a central location in the network is a necessary condition to opinion leadership since it relates directly to the opportunity to influence others. How one should think about "centrality" is less obvious. Most marketers and market research firms appear to do so in terms of degree centrality. A refinement might be to think not only about direct contacts, but also about how many actors can be reached in two or three steps—an idea more akin to closeness centrality. However, in network structures with dense subgroups that are loosely interconnected, which is how many human networks are structured, the actors linking the subgroups—that is, spanning structural holes—may be critical. Moreover, these bridges are likely to be exposed to more and unique information. Such actors would qualify as "cosmopolitan" rather than "local" opinion leaders (Merton 1949, 1968). One of us has analyzed a social network of physicians in which the identity of the most degree-central physicians was well known to the pharmaceutical firm sponsoring the study. However, the finding that there were two large subgroups, one consisting mostly of physicians with names of European origin and the other mostly of physicians with names of Asian origin, was an eye-opener. Even more surprising was the finding that only three physicians bridged these two subgroups. One of these physicians had the highest betweenness centrality in the network and had until then been ignored by the medical education and sales teams of the firm.

Ideal opinion leaders engage in many conversations about new products. However, this characteristic cannot be assumed to be present in all opinion leaders. Some may have a missionary zeal about sharing their opinions, but others may be more reserved and selective. Obviously, the former are more valuable as seeding points.

The number of conversations customers engage in is a function not only of their network providing the opportunity to influence others, but also of how interesting the message is and, hence, how high the motivation to share it with others. P&G's Vocalpoint word-of-mouth marketing program, for instance, focuses on recruiting homemakers with large social networks, but also does quite a bit of research to find what motivates these homemakers to share the information with their friends and acquaintances (Berner 2006). Also, when the cost of sharing the information is high, opinion leaders may be reluctant to share information with anyone but their strong ties. Frenzen and Nakamoto (1993) document such selectivity in sharing information when its value decreases as more people receive it, like information about a secret sale in a store or about where to buy a hard-to-find prestigious product.

Our review of social contagion and opinion leadership is purposely critical, as many beliefs circulating in the marketing community are unfounded in, or even run contrary to, empirical research findings. Our framing of the issues will help marketers ask pertinent questions before embarking on marketing campaigns for new products. In the appendix, we mention two books written by practitioners and two by academics that flesh out the issues further.

Buzz Marketing As we have discussed, most marketing efforts that exploit network structure attempt to leverage centrally located opinion leaders. However, as also noted, network centrality is only one characteristic of the ideal opinion leader; the pattern of ties is far less central in several other types of word-of-mouth (WOM) marketing, usually called "buzz marketing." Buzz marketing might be described as word-of-mouth marketing that does not exploit the network structure.

Buzz marketing typically refers to marketing communications that aim to grab attention in the media and among consumers. Well-known examples include Apple Computer's "1984" TV ad, apparel retailer French Connection UK's plastering its store windows and shopping bags with its acronym FCUK, Internet retailer Half.com paying the small town of Halfway, Oregon to rename itself Half.com for a year, and Burger King's "Subservient Chicken" website.

Buzz marketing seeks to develop creative content that is so unusual, hilarious, taboo, or otherwise remarkable that a media effort gets leveraged in the press and in conversations among consumers (e.g., Hughes 2005; Salzman, Matathia, and O'Reilly 2003). The structure of the network does not come into play in such a campaign.

One would expect buzz marketing to be effective in generating awareness. In some cases, it might also be effective in building strong beliefs and attitudes towards the brand. However, the ability of buzz marketing to convert positive attitudes into actual purchases may not be much higher than traditional marketing communications, especially for expensive and risky products where endorsements from opinion leaders or actual users can be critical. In those cases, one may want to follow Silverman's (2001) advice and use traditional marketing media to provide information about the product, but "use word of mouth to present confirmation and verification of the information" (p. 203).

Some buzz marketers put less emphasis on noteworthy marketing communications campaigns. One such firm is BzzAgent which, like P&G's Tremor and Vocalpoint, gives away the product for free in the hope that the recipients will generate positive WOM. Unlike Tremor and Vocalpoint, however, the BzzAgent service is predicated on the idea that network structure is not critical. The assumption is that everyone spreads WOM provided they're enthusiastic (or deeply disappointed) about the product (Balter and Butman 2005). That assumption is quite reasonable, as is the assumption that people with extensive ties will reach a larger audience. From a managerial point of view, it is a question of efficiency: Do the efforts in identifying and selectively targeting well-connected consumers create a return that is sufficiently higher than not using network structure when distributing samples?

Campaigns like those by BzzaAgent furthermore assume that WOM generators need not be trendsetters or innovators. That too is reasonable, and is consistent with prior research findings. Still, it is equally reasonable to expect that people who are recognized as experts will be more credible and persuasive (provided that their level of expertise is not so high that their usage experience becomes irrelevant for most consumers). So, the question managers must ask is: Who are the relevant social sources for the message we want to convey to our target audience? For highly complex products early in their commercial life, the only credible sources may be experts and leading-edge users. Later on, as the firm seeks adoption by the mass market, experts with national recognition may be less effective than local users who are seen as more representative and credible by those mainstream customers who have not adopted yet (e.g., Moore 1991). For more "mundane" products, representativeness may trump expertise as early as the day of launch.

In short, not every type of word-of-mouth marketing exploits network structure. Whether or not that is an advantage from a marketing efficiency point of view is likely to depend on one's marketing objectives, the nature of the product, and the stage of the diffusion cycle.

Viral Marketing Viral marketing is often used as a synonym for word-of-mouth marketing, but typically refers more specifically to online word-of-mouth activities. Our opinion is that so far, most viral marketing has focused on contagion dynamics while ignoring network structure. This is ironic, since many marketers got interested in social networks only when extensive use of the Internet ushered in the "age of connectedness." To clarify, let us look at three well-known examples of viral marketing. In the first, email service provider Hotmail cleverly appended a little message advertising its service to all outgoing mail from its users (Rosen 2000). Clearly, Hotmail used all "nodes" and "links" of that network but without any particular attention to network structure (rightly so, given the zero cost and 100% transfer rate). The second example is offered by application software like Adobe Acrobat where the value of using the product increases with the number of others using the product or close complements. Despite the fact that they are taking advantage of "network effects," marketers of software products do not seem to care very much about network structure, focusing instead on the size and growth of the installed base. (Exceptions may be B2B markets where the endorsement of a very few key reference accounts can make a big difference.) The third example is marketers' current enthusiasm for "social networking" sites as locations where they can reach teenagers (via MySpace and Facebook) and other audiences that are increasingly hard to reach via TV advertising. Many such marketing efforts seem to be little more than traditional advertising spiffed up with more user interactivity. The pattern of links among the site members does not seem to be the focus of much marketing concern.

Recent developments in Web technology and practices suggest that viral marketers may soon pay more attention to the pattern of online connections among consumers. The primary reason is the availability of data which may allow marketers to differentiate consumers who are critical in spreading information and consumers who are influential. For instance, with its acquisition of Internet telephony upstart Skype, eBay now has data on who talks to whom. Similarly, gmail provides Google data on consumer interrelationships which it is already using for marketing purposes. True network-based marketing campaigns might be a next step. Hill, Provost, and Volinsky (2006) report on an application of network-based marketing during the launch of a new telecommunications service at AT&T. Users of the Epinions product review website can now build a "Web of Trust" of reviewers whose comments and ratings they have consistently found to be valuable. Another development is social bookmarking or tagging (e.g., BlinkList, del.icio.us, Furl, Spurl), where users can gain access to their friends' archives and receive a daily email of the websites their friends found interesting enough to tag. Such developments may lead viral marketers to focus more on network structure, since data on who considers whom a source of valuable information may allow one to differentiate members critical in the spread of information and influence.

Social Influence and Existing Brands

Information Dissemination Much of what we have discussed about social contagion in new product contexts also applies to existing products, though the effects tend to be weaker. For existing products, creating awareness is less important, as is educating customers about product characteristics and benefits. Since there is less novel information to share about established products, opinion leaders are less motivated to discuss them. However, even established products have a changing potential customer base. This is especially true for products consumed by relatively specific age groups. Every year, millions of teenagers get interested in products they did not care about before, millions of adults become first-time parents or first-time home-owners, millions of adults start planning for life after retirement, and so on. Like potential new product adopters, these novice customers must go through a multi-step process to overcome the hurdles to product adoption.

Casual empiricism suggests that word-of-mouth referrals may also be important for professional services with high financial or health risk, even when websites and other sources provide supposedly objective and relevant information about different providers. Referrals may even be the sole source of information for professional services for which the market is so small that no objective information is provided in any mass media channel, like piano tuners (Reingen and Kernan 1986) or piano teachers (Brown and Reingen 1987).

Although few studies of interpersonal influence in the context of established products have used social network data, the little empirical evidence that is available is mostly consistent with basic theory. For instance, in a study of referral networks for piano teachers, Brown and Reingen (1987) find that people looking for referrals were more likely to activate strong ties than weak ties, but that activated weak ties were more likely to serve as conduits through which novel information became available. This is consistent with the "strength of weak ties" argument. Yet, consistent with the notion that strong ties are more trustworthy, recipients tended to be more influenced by strong tie referrals then weak tie referrals.

Brand Preference "Brand congruence," or the extent to which strongly connected consumers have similar brand preferences, has attracted some attention among consumer researchers. Social cohesion arguments, especially balance theory, imply that people who are strongly tied to each other are likely to exhibit similar brand preferences. Having a structurally equivalent position has also been associated with having similar brand preferences (Ward and Reingen 1990). While several studies document a link between having ties to particular reference groups and having similar brand use or brand preference (e.g., Bearden and Etzel 1982; Childers and Rao 1992; Witt and Bruce 1970; Stafford 1966), hardly any evidence of such effects exist at the level of dyadic ties. One exception is a study by Reingen et al. (1984) which finds a positive association between common membership in a cohesive subgroup (49 female college students who were members of the same sorority) and common brand use or brand preference. Moreover, the authors measure network ties for 10 different relationships (roommate, friend, studying together, etc.) and find significantly greater brand congruence for multiplex subgroups, i.e., subgroups that occurred in several different relations, than for relation-specific subgroups. This study, however, does not allow one to conclude that brand congruence resulted from cohesion, since it is likely that both are affected by similarity in tastes and values, which was not controlled for. Also, as the authors note, the majority of the significant findings stemmed from only 3 of the 16 products studied, and all three—TV show, restaurant, and pizza—are often consumed jointly in interpersonal settings. Other products for which significant findings were identified, like shampoo and magazines, are also often shared by students living in close proximity. Finally, the fact that the subjects were members of the same sorority casts doubt on the extent to which the strength of the associations found in this study generalizes to less cohesive or less other-directed parts of the general population (Park and Lessig 1977). This study raises the question about how weak particular ties can become before losing their effectiveness, and how this varies across customer groups (e.g., teenagers and college kids vs. adults). Unfortunately, we are not aware of relevant research on this issue.

Other studies on brand congruence did not study network ties explicitly, yet produced four results worth mentioning here. First, several studies document that people differ in their susceptibility to interpersonal influence, and that this susceptibility has two dimensions. The first is informational: the tendency to learn about products and services by observing others or seeking information from others. The second is normative, and captures both (1) a willingness to conform to the expectations of others regarding purchase decisions and (2) a desire to identify with or enhance one's image in the opinion of significant others through the acquisition and use of products and brands (e.g., Bearden, Netemeyer, and Teel 1989; Burnkrant and Cousineau 1975; Deutsch and Gerard 1955).

The second result pertains to differences among products. One would expect that social influence is greater when consumers face social risk and, consequently, greater for product and brand decisions involving conspicuous products. In line with such expectations, Witt and Bruce (1970) find that brand choice congruence within groups is greater for cigarettes and beer than for deodorant. In a more thorough study, Bearden and Etzel (1982) find that interpersonal influence is greater for publicly consumed products than for privately consumed products, and greater for luxuries than for necessities. In addition, value-expressive normative influence is greater for category-level decisions than for brand-level decisions, whereas informational influence is about equally important for the two kinds of decisions. More recently, Berger and Heath (2007) illustrate that interpersonal influence strongly affects congruence even in categories, products, and behaviors that are less conspicuous (e.g., music tastes), as long as people see them as markers of social identity.

The third finding on brand congruence that is relevant to our discussion pertains to group cohesiveness. Stafford (1966) finds that the cohesiveness of a group (operationalized not as density but as the average valence of the ties within the group) has no direct effect on brand choice. However, the probability that members prefer the same brand as the group's leader is much higher in cohesive than in noncohesive groups. "Thus," Stafford concludes, "cohesiveness appeared to have its most important function in providing an agreeable environment in which informal leaders could effectively operate" (p. 74). We are not aware of any replications of this result.

Finally, structural balance theory implies that interpersonal influence need not always lead to congruence and imitation. It can also lead to the opposite. When someone you dislike or want to distinguish yourself from likes a product, you are more likely to dislike the product. People have been documented to avoid products associated with out-group members and even to abandon products they are using once out-group members adopted them (Berger and Heath 2007; Bourdieu 1984; Simmel 1950).

Brand Beliefs A third area where social networks may be relevant to marketing existing products and brands is the extent to which people who interact socially tend to have similar product and brand cognitions. Thus, it would be of great interest to understand how social networks relate to brand cultures. Unfortunately, this area has not attracted the attention of consumer researchers. The only relevant study we are aware is one by Sirsi, Ward, and Reingen (1996) on social networks and cognitive networks among animal rights activists and macrobiotics enthusiasts. They report that social integration and sharing of cognitive structures are related among the animal rights activists. Among the adherents of macrobiotics, who are a more mainstream and less radical set of individuals than the animal rights activists, associations between social ties and cognitive network similarities exist among the members of a subgroup consisting mostly of experts, but not among the members of a subgroup consisting mostly of novices. Overall, these results seem to suggest that the link between social interaction and cognitive structure is strong among hard-core enthusiasts of particular consumption ideologies but not among less committed adherents. This makes intuitive sense, but raises questions about the extent to which such connections exist for commercial brands, with the possible exception of iconic brands with some extreme enthusiasts among their customer base.

Transaction Networks

A key problem that buyers and sellers face is uncertainty about the trustworthiness of their counter-parties (e.g., product availability and quality, prompt payment, delivery, etc.). Consumers buying and selling amongst themselves have long used third parties to reduce that uncertainty by establishing escrow accounts, providing information on seller reliability, and so on. The real estate market is an example. EBay and other e-commerce operators replicate this intermediary role, thus reducing transaction cost (and getting remunerated for it). However, relational and structural embeddedness in existing networks may obviate the need for commercial third parties. Using interview data from over 1,400 respondents to the 1996 General Social Survey, DiMaggio and Louch (1998) find that when people make significant purchases from other consumers rather than commercial establishments, 20% to 40% do so from people with whom they have prior noncommercial relationships, either directly (relatives, friends, or acquaintances) or via a common link (friend of a friend, relative of a friend, etc.). Theory suggests that transacting with social contacts is effective because it embeds commercial exchanges in a web of obligations and holds the seller's network hostage to appropriate role performance in the economic transaction. This implies that exchanges within one's extended ego-network will be more common for risky transactions that are unlikely to be repeated and in which uncertainty is high. DiMaggio and Louch's data support this prediction. Exchange frequency reduces the extent to which one uses parties from within one's extended ego-network. Further, their findings support the argument that uncertainty about product and performance quality leads people to prefer sellers with whom they have direct or indirect noncommercial ties. Moreover, people who transact with friends and relatives report greater satisfaction with the results than do people who transact with strangers, especially for risk-laden exchanges.

Several of the contingencies mentioned in our discussion of social contagion are likely to be relevant to consumer-to-consumer transaction networks as well. One example is the reliance on networks for products that are illicit or otherwise taboo (e.g., Lee 1969).

While such findings on consumer-to-consumer transactions may not be of immediate interest to most marketing managers, they corroborate several of the theoretical ideas discussed in the chapter on social capital and illustrate how they can affect consumer behavior.

5

Intra-organizational Networks

Networks exist not only among customers, but also within the firm. We discuss four intra-organizational issues of particular relevance to marketers for which research documents a link to network structure: power, dissemination of knowledge (especially in the context of innovation), employee recruitment and turnover, and industrial buying behavior.

Our review is selective in that it focuses on consequences rather than antecedents of network structure, and then only on consequences of particular interest to marketers. Management researchers have identified many variables affecting the structure of interpersonal networks within organizations. In essence, homophily, physical distance, and location in the formal organization are key determinants, none of which is very surprising. Management researchers have also documented effects that networks have on both individuals and larger subgroups such as departments but are not of direct relevance to marketers. For reviews, one can consult papers by Brass et al. (2004), Krackhardt and Brass (1994), and Raider and Krackhardt (2002).

Power

It is a core belief among marketers that, for the organization to succeed, it must be market oriented. To influence their organization to act in a market-oriented fashion, marketers need power. Unsurprisingly, power is associated with central network positions in workflow, advice, and friendship networks. The three most common graph-theoretic measures of centrality—degree, closeness (capturing access), and betweenness (capturing information control)—have all been related to power. In addition, closeness to the dominant players in the firm is shown to be strongly related to both power and promotion (for a review, see Brass et al. [2004]). An important caveat for much of this research, however, is that most studies do not establish cause and effect: Does centrality lead to power, or does power lead to centrality because others want to befriend or gain access to powerful actors? In this regard, a longitudinal study by Burkhardt and Brass (1992) shows that centrality preceded power in the company they studied. The causal effect has also been documented in laboratory experiments.

Merely being perceived to have powerful alters is also important. Kilduff and Krackhardt (1994) find that, in the small entrepreneurial firm they studied, being perceived to have a prominent friend was associated with an individual's reputation as a good performer, but that actually having such a friend had no such relation. (The signaling value of one's partners matters in inter-organizational networks as well, and is discussed further in the next chapter.)

Conversely, having accurate perceptions of the actual network structure is also related to power, according to a study in what appears to be the same small entrepreneurial firm (Krackhardt 1990). Those who had a more accurate mental picture of the overall advice network were rated as more powerful by others in the organization, even though having an accurate mental picture of the friendship network was not related to reputational power.

Disseminating Market Knowledge within the Firm

It is commonly understood that, for the organization to be market oriented, market knowledge must be shared and disseminated throughout the firm. Research to date has emphasized the role of formal information systems, formal integrative management processes, organizational structures, incentives and rewards, personnel movement, and corporate culture in this dissemination process (e.g., Griffin and Hauser 1996). There is little research on the role of social networks in disseminating market information, and most existing research pertains to the innovation process where combining technical and market information is critical (e.g., Griffin and Hauser 1992; Moenaert and Souder 1990). We discuss some of the more relevant network studies in the context of innovation below.

Another area of interest is how marketers learn about their markets. Here again, most research emphasizes formal means of disseminating knowledge, like market research reports and market information systems. Little is known about the extent and manner in which marketers' networks affect their market knowledge and actions. One study points at the complexities that may be involved. Mizruchi and Stearns (2001) examine the means by which relationship managers in a major commercial bank attempted to close transactions with their corporate customers. The researchers hypothesized that under conditions of high uncertainty, bankers would rely on colleagues with whom they are strongly tied for advice on and support of their deals. However, based on information redundancy arguments, they also hypothesized that transactions in which bankers used relatively sparse approval networks would be more likely to successfully close than transactions involving dense approval networks. Both hypotheses were supported with the net outcome that these relationship managers were faced with a strategic paradox: their tendency to rely on those they trust in dealing with uncertainty created conditions that rendered deals less likely to be closed successfully. This paradox between strong tie and weak ties, and between closure and structural holes, will come up again when we discuss the flow of ideas in the context of innovation management.

Innovation and the Flow of Ideas A central finding in the innovation literature is that novel ideas often come from people in a boundary-spanning position, i.e., people who connect their formal unit, like department or firm, to the outside world. This pattern has been documented quite extensively and thoroughly for R&D teams (Allen 1977), but is also reported in a strategy initiative involving actors from multiple departments (Hutt, Reingen, and Ronchetto 1988). In network terms, formal units often coincide with relatively dense subgroups in the communication network, and people with boundary-spanning positions have high betweenness centrality and span structural holes between their unit/subgroup and the rest of the network. In other words, the classic finding on boundary-spanning positions is consistent with the theoretical notion that actors with high betweenness centrality play an important role in the flow of ideas.[20] As Tushman and Katz (1980) and Obstfeld (2005) observe, people in such boundary-spanning and brokerage positions do not necessarily try to control the flow of information to their own benefit. They may also simply act as mediators or matchmakers bringing people together in projects. Hence, their importance can be greater than their continued involvement in projects would suggest.

To mobilize resources necessary to get a project or strategy initiative off the ground, being on the periphery of one's unit is not necessarily an asset (e.g., Tushman and Romanelli 1983). More important is the ability to influence others to support the project or initiative with the resources at their disposal. Here, strong ties to many actors (degree centrality in strong ties), access to many other actors in the network, especially through strong ties (closeness centrality in strong ties), and the quality and quantity of alters' resources are important. A study of an Internet initiative in a *Fortune* 500 company supports this theory-based prediction: closeness centrality in the networks of workflow interactions, friendship, and advice was positively associated with the extent to which managers were seen as being effective at their jobs (even after controlling for leadership positions), whereas betweenness centrality was not (Bond et al. 2004).

Further insights on the role of strong versus weak ties and on closure versus reaching across structural holes come from several studies that use the project rather than the manager as their unit of analysis. As we noted in chapters 2 and 3, strong ties can be especially valuable to convey complex knowledge for two reasons: they provide a stronger motivation to exert effort necessary for such transfers, and they increase the ability to do so. On the other hand, the strength-of-weak-tie argument suggests that strong ties may be less effective in locating novel information. This leads to a "search-transfer problem": weak ties are good for search, strong ties are better for transfer, and there is no easy answer to the question, "Which is best?" This dilemma is confirmed by Hansen (1999) in a network study of 120 new product development projects undertaken by 41 divisions in a large electronics company. He finds that weak inter-unit ties indeed help a project team search for useful knowledge in other subunits but impede the transfer of complex knowledge. Importantly, and as one would expect based on theory, he also finds that knowledge complexity determines which effect dominates: having weak inter-unit ties speeds up search-transfer when knowledge is not complex but slows it down when the knowledge is highly complex.

Reagans and McEvily (2003) investigate three aspects of social capital discussed above: (1) strong ties help convey complex knowledge, (2) closure or local clustering affect the willingness and motivation of individuals to invest time, energy, and effort in sharing knowledge with others, and (3) lack of redundancy, i.e., access to loosely connected subgroups, leads to a greater ability to tap into nonoverlapping pools of knowledge and also a greater reliability in one's interpretation of information received. They analyze 1,518 project teams in a contract research and development firm, and find that teams with high closure among the team members but low closure among the team members' outside contacts tended to complete projects faster. These effects are found to operate over and above the effect of tie strength. Hence, this study documents that the network structure affects innovation even after taking into account the strength of the individual ties. Also, the study shows not only that having local closure and bridging a structural hole can both be beneficial, but also that, like in the small world situation, these two network characteristics are not mutually exclusive. Combining local closure among many of one's contacts (e.g., team members) with a lack of redundancy among one's remaining contacts combines the benefits of both at the same time. An earlier study of 224 R&D teams in 29 corporations in 7 industries reports the same result: closure and nonredundancy both boost innovation performance, and they can be achieved simultaneously (Reagans and Zuckerman 2001). Further corroboration of the idea of a "sweet spot" combining local closure and nonredundancy comes from a study of the financial and artistic success of Broadway musicals from 1945 to 1989 (Uzzi and Spiro 2005).

There is no theoretical reason to expect that these results would be specific to the innovation context. A meta-analysis of 37 studies of teams in a variety of natural contexts suggests there is no empirical reason either (Balkundi and Harrison 2006). Teams with densely configured interpersonal ties attained their goals better and were more committed to staying together. This finding is consistent with the closure argument. Further, teams with leaders who were central in the teams' intra-group networks and teams that were central in their inter-group network tend to perform better. Both findings, and especially the latter, are consistent with the structural hole argument.

The theoretical arguments and empirical findings that internal closure and external reach are both important for innovation have implications for how to manage team diversity in the context of innovation. Given that people's network alters often share their demographic attributes (i.e., the network is homophilous), increasing a team's demographic diversity should increase the team's social range (as it will cross-cut several social circles through its members) but decrease the team's internal density. When forming teams, one must hence look beyond mere demographic diversity and look at the members' social connections, since the latter ultimately relate more directly to the causal mechanisms affecting team performance (Reagans, Zuckerman, and McEvily 2004).

Organizing for Creativity and Innovation For generating and exploiting innovative products and ideas, social networks matter not only at the project level, but also at the corporate level.

A classic example is the Xerox Palo Alto Research Center (PARC) which was launched in the 1970s as a center aimed at creating the new architecture of information. PARC was highly successful in generating creative ideas, prototypes, and product concepts (such as the first personal computer, the first graphical user interface, the first mouse, and the Ethernet). However, it operated independently from corporate headquarters and from the commercial divisions. The distance between PARC near San Francisco and the Xerox headquarters in Connecticut and the Office Products Division in Dallas compounded the differences in technological expertise, professional values, and lifestyles between PARC employees and others in Xerox—quite the opposite of integration through cross-cutting social circles. As a result, PARC failed to build the required commitment within Xerox to commercialize their visionary innovations (e.g., Smith and Alexander 1988).

3M exemplifies a more successful endeavor, using what might be called "technology brokering." After the discovery of a novel technology called microreplication, 3M created the Optical Technology Center to find and develop new applications of this and related technologies. OTC acted as a technology broker in that it spanned different businesses within 3M and transferred ideas from their origination to new application areas, resulting in an impressive list of creative innovations throughout the company (Hargadon 2003). By identifying the need for bridging ties, and creating those through the means of a new node in the form of OTC, 3M was able to boost commercial innovation.

Communities of practice are a less formal way to achieve similar benefits (e.g., Brown and Duguid 1991, 2001). The basic idea is that each firm should recognize itself as a constellation of communities, where each community is defined by the

similarity of the activities that are performed by its members. As knowledge is sel-
dom perfectly transferable in blueprints, especially when it concerns how things
ought to be done or when it relates to complex technologies, joint practice is the
natural way to share such knowledge with others. Defining ties on the basis of par-
ticipation in similar activities can be very useful for fostering knowledge flows
within the organization (Cross and Parker 2004). Specifically, by identifying the
similarity in activities performed, one can gain insight into who would benefit
from interacting with whom, and identify opportunities for people to form active
communities of practice.

Employee Recruitment and Turnover

Finding and keeping good employees is rarely seen as falling within the purview of
marketing. However, as noted in Chapter 1, employee retention is important to
marketers in service industries where employees interact directly with the customer and have a major impact on quality and customer satisfaction.

Using the insight that network ties can be important to help people find jobs,
some employers have instituted formal network referral programs where current
employees suggest friends or acquaintances as job applicants. In principle, network
referrals can provide employers with a richer pool of applicants, better matches
between applicants and job requirements (including temperament and fit with culture), and a ready-made source of social support by the referees once the applicants
are hired. In an extremely detailed analysis of such a program in a call center,
Fernandez, Castilla, and Moore (2000) find that, taking into account costs of initial application screening, subsequent interviewing, and differences in odds of pro-
ceeding from the initial application to job acceptance, the company realized $417
costs savings with referrals—representing a 67% return on the $250 referral bonus
paid to referees. In another study of a call center, Castilla (2005) finds that referral-
hires were initially more productive than nonreferral-hires. More surprisingly, he
also finds that referral hires exhibited higher performance and attachment to the
firm well beyond the time of hiring.

A pair of studies by Krackhardt and Porter (1985, 1986) in a restaurant business
looks at network effects on employee turnover. In their first study, they find evidence of social contagion in employee turnover: people were more likely to leave
after others with a similar position in the advice network had done so. This suggests that people considered not their direct contacts (advisors or advisees) but
those in a similar position as providing more relevant information about the
nature of their jobs and about alternatives to working at that particular restaurant
chain. Investigating the effects of turnover on those who decided to remain,
Krackhardt and Porter find—rather surprisingly—that those who were friends of

leavers became significantly more satisfied and committed to the organization after their friends had left than those who were not friends with the leavers. The authors suggest a "rotten apple" theory to explain this: people considering leaving were unhappy and, before leaving, shared their disgruntlement with their friends. After they left, however, their friends who stayed were not subjected anymore to that source of negative affect, and so started liking their employer more. This is, in essence, nothing more than an application of balance theory, but a rather unexpected one.

Over the last 15 years marked by downsizing, delayering, and re-engineering, employees have become increasingly interested in networking to advance their own career within and beyond the firm, as evidenced by the success of self-help books with titles like *Networking Smart* and *Achieving Success through Social Capital* (Baker 1994, 2000). Human resources and even legal departments have also become interested in networks, as evidence suggests that women and ethnic minorities may suffer a disadvantage—not necessarily through any formal policies discriminating against them, but simply by a network structure that makes it less easy to use informal sources of information, support, and influence (e.g., Burt 1998; Ibarra 1992, 1995; Laird 2006). Of particular interest to marketers is a recent finding that not only employees' networks but also the customer portfolio of the firm itself may affect career patterns. Beckman and Philips (2005) find that law firms with corporate clients having women in positions of leadership (CEO, board director, or general counsel) were more likely to promote women attorneys than other law firms. In other words, the inter-firm network of customers—something clearly within the purview of marketers—may affect how minorities fare within the organization itself. Network theory suggests that this effect occurs as a result of "homophily" and "structural balance," concepts explained in Chapter 2.

Industrial Buying

Unlike other areas where intra-organizational networks have been studied, industrial buying behavior is one area where marketing rather than management scholars or sociologists have done the more relevant research. Since we are not aware of any review article on social networks in industrial buying processes, we cover this area in greater detail than the other issues in this chapter.

Complex purchasing decisions almost always involve several participants who collectively make up the "decision-making unit" (DMU) or "buying center" for the purchase decision. In contrast to what one might expect, these participants need not interact much with each other or ever meet all together, as Cyert, Simon, and Trow (1956) observe in an early case study. The DMU need not have the formal status of a task force or ad hoc committee within the firm, and individual members need not even define themselves as members of such an informal group. In this sense, DMUs certainly do not constitute a cohesive group (Bristor and Ryan 1987). As a result, identifying the actors involved in the purchase decision can be difficult and may require extensive snowballing, asking each member one has identified so far the question, "Who else is involved?" (e.g., Moriarty 1983).

We do not know very much about how these DMU members interrelate as a network. Five positions or roles are typically posited (buyer, decider, influencer, gatekeeper, and user), but that is a minimal list and many more may exist. Calder (1977) suggests up to 25 roles. The truth of the matter is that roles are an underdeveloped part of network theory in general, and we have very little empirical knowledge about roles in industrial buying situations in particular. Several studies claiming to study network structure do not really do so because they do not analyze the pattern of ties. One example is a study by Dawes and Lee (1996) where DMU members were asked to report some actor attributes (hierarchical level and departmental affiliation) of themselves and other members of the DMU, but not to provide any information on their ties with other DMU members. Johnston and Bonoma (1981) similarly reduce the "structure and interaction patterns" of the DMU to five dimensions rather than collecting and analyzing actual network data on the pattern of communication among DMU members. This procedure has the advantage that one can limit oneself to interviewing just a few key informants per DMU, rather than each participant, but does not provide insights into the network structure itself (Iacobucci and Hopkins 1992). Still, a handful of studies do provide some insight on the network structure of DMUs. As we discuss next, they document how centrality in the informal network, associated with control of the information flow, is associated with influence on decisions.

The DMU as a Network In a single case study, Calder (1977) used directed network graphs to illustrate how the set of tasks and actors were interrelated and could be interpreted as roles or positions in structurally isomorphic networks. His early proposal to use structural role analysis to study industrial buying behavior, however, has not been followed up on, perhaps because this has long been a conceptually and technically challenging area of network analysis (see Borgatti and Everett 1992 for a useful review).

In a quantitative study of four DMUs, Bristor (1993) finds that being centrally and widely connected throughout the organization enabled DMU members to access needed resources for effective influence attempts, such as support and information. Her study also confirms that influence was exerted not only by advocacy but also by gatekeeping, as emphasized by structural hole theory.

Similarly, in a study of 41 DMUs, Dawes, Lee, and Dowling (1998) find that a member's betweenness centrality in the DMU had a significant impact on his or her influence on the selection of a supplier. This effect was still detectable and significant after controlling for several other factors, including how big a stake the member held in the decision, how highly involved the person was in the process, how original his or her ideas were, and how highly formalized and centralized the firm was. The researchers also investigate how betweenness centrality was associated with other variables. They find that people who had a larger stake and were more involved in the decision were also more central. This suggests, yet doesn't demonstrate, that actors might be able to purposely increase their centrality in the information flow pertaining to decisions they care about. People with more original ideas also tended to be more central, but here causality is even less clear.

All the previous studies took the DMU for a specific purchase decision as their unit of analysis. Ronchetto, Hutt, and Reingen (1989), in contrast, looked at 171 employees of a firm who participated in buying-related workflows or communications. From this, they constructed two networks, one for workflow and one for communications. In each network, degree, closeness, and betweenness centrality were highly correlated ($r = .7$ or higher), so the researchers collapsed them into a single factor. Centrality scores were also highly correlated across the workflow and the communication network, so the researchers collapsed them into a single score. As in previous studies, centrality was positively associated with influence, even after controlling for departmental affiliation, formal rank (positive effect on influence), path distance from people outside the organization providing relevant information (negative effect), and path distance from members of the top management team who were rated as especially influential in the buying decisions (negative effect). So, position in the network was important in several ways: not only centrality within the group mattered, but also the extent to which one had control over the inflow of outside information and the extent to which one was close to key influentials. This multiplicity of effects is consistent with the idea that social capital is not a monolithic, but a multi-faceted, concept.

Crossing the Firm's Boundaries The relevant network in the industrial buying process need not be confined within the firm but can cross firm boundaries. In a study of almost 200 paper-buying firms, Martilla (1971) finds that the employees involved in buying decisions engaged in a fair amount of word-of-mouth communication both within their own firm and with peers in competing firms. About 30% reported talking with peers outside their firm early in the adoption process, and this proportion increased to about 50% in the later stages. Hence, just as in consumer markets, word-of-mouth was more important in the later stages of the decision-making process. Interestingly, there was no difference in the amount of opinion seeking within one's own firm versus competing firms. So, word-of-mouth easily crossed firm boundaries in this sample. It did so especially among envelope-making firms typically serving regional markets and offering relatively standardized products. In contrast, very little information was shared among greeting card companies, which served the national market and competed on design creativity rather than price and delivery. Hence, one must be careful to generalize about the amount of information sharing among competing firms. As common sense suggests and this study supports, whether or not competitive considerations preclude sharing information about purchased products is strongly related to the intensity of rivalry among them. Still, since interfirm contacts have been observed in several studies and industries, it appears safe to use as baseline assumption that such contacts are likely to exist (e.g., Czepiel 1974).

Martilla (1971) also finds that opinion leaders were more exposed to impersonal sources of information than other buying influentials in the firm were. This is consistent with the two-step flow hypothesis mentioned in our discussion of opinion leadership in Chapter 4.

In a smaller study of 58 firms, Webster (1970) similarly finds that buying firms engaged in a fair amount of communication with other buying firms. About 20% of the respondents reported talking with buyers in other firms; this percentage remained constant across the awareness, interest, and evaluation stages. More respondents reported talking to other firms' engineers, and this fraction increased from about 25% at the awareness stage, to about 35% at the interest stage, to about 45% at the evaluation stage. Respondents were unanimous in reporting that they would not contact anyone previously unknown to them when searching for information. They limited their search mostly to nearby firms. Unsurprisingly, the regional association of purchasing professionals seemed to play an important role in acquainting purchasing people with one another. Several other studies that document the presence and effects of inter-organizational networks are discussed in the next chapter.

In short, existing network research into industrial buying indicates that industrial marketers and salespeople who understand the informal network within the DMU will better understand who the true influentials are, and how information and influence from outside the firm can seep into the DMU and must be reckoned with.

6

Inter-organizational Networks

As noted earlier, the potential benefits of social capital include improved coordination, access to resources, control over the flow of resources, and status. These benefits also apply to networks in which firms and other organizations, rather than consumers or employees, are the nodes. In this chapter, we focus on five substantive areas where the structure of inter-organizational networks matters: coordinating channels, accessing resources through alliances, gaining status, managing competition, and adopting new suppliers, technologies, and practices.

Coordinating Channels

Most existing knowledge on channel coordination stems from dyadic research. Two issues have been studied extensively: (1) power and conflict and (2) the development of long-term relationships over time. Until the late 1980s, most research applied ideas from social psychology and social exchange theory to channel dyads (e.g., Emerson 1962; Thibaut and Kelly 1959). Subsequent applications of the transaction cost approach (Williamson 1975, 1985) to issues of inter-organizational coordination strengthened the focus on the isolated dyadic transaction. Game-theoretical analyses go beyond dyads, but focus only on very stylized network structures. As a result, we know much about dyadic-relational issues such as relational affect and attitudes, relationship continuity and trust, personal attachments, the history of inter-firm cooperation, and coordination failures due to poor incentive alignment, but very little about how these issues are affected by network structure. Further, there has been virtually no attention in channel research to the network exchange literature developed in the late 1980s and 1990s (Cook and Whitmeyer 1992; Markovsky, Willer, and Patton 1988). This is rather odd, since this stream of theory and research focuses on coordination and conflict issues, with particular attention to power (e.g., Skvoretz and Willer 1993) and justice (e.g., Molm, Quist, and Wiseley 1994)—issues that channel researchers have studied for decades from a purely dyadic perspective.

Few marketing studies have examined the governance implications of triadic or network structures. A recent exception is Wathne and Heide's (2004) examination of the fashion apparel industry in which they surveyed both apparel companies and their retailer-customers. They find that apparel companies' efforts in qualifying and selecting their upstream suppliers increased their ability to accommodate uncertainty in the downstream market. Another exception is an experimental study of computer network buyers by Wuyts et al. (2004). They find that buyers' preference for strong ties with their systems integrators varied as a function of these vendors' portfolio of upstream ties to suppliers. Both studies point to the need to go beyond dyadic accounts when thinking about channel structure and coordination issues. Below, we discuss why networks matter in terms of channel coordination.

Network Structure Effects on Coordination Network closure supports several mechanisms relevant to channel coordination: boosting reputational effects, boosting the emergence of cooperative norms, and diminishing the possibility of exploitative brokering. Two-step leverage is a fourth mechanism we discuss, but one that does not require closure.

Closure and reputation As is well known from the "Iterated Prisoners' Dilemma" and similar game-theoretical problems, efficient cooperation between two actors is more likely to occur when each knows and remembers the other's prior actions (e.g., Axelrod 1984). The same idea applies to situations where a focal actor plays the game repeatedly with a different counterpart in every round, but where the focal actor's alters have high closure so they can share information about the focal actor (e.g., Raub and Weesie 1990). Buyers can communicate the supplier's opportunistic exploitation to other potential buyers (Macaulay 1963; Raub and Weesie 1990), and thus, damage the supplier's reputation as a trustworthy exchange partner (Dollinger, Golden, and Saxton 1997) and eventually even cause the supplier to lose future contracts (Greif 1993; Houston and Johnson 2000). This reputation mechanism is most effective when information is easily communicated throughout the network, i.e., when network density and network centrality are high (Buskens 1998).[21] In this regard, Antia and Frazier (2001) survey 213 managers in franchisor organizations and investigate the effect of franchisees' network density and centrality on how severely the franchisor enforces the contract in the case of contract violations. They find that enforcement is weaker in cases of higher density and centrality. Their interpretation is that other network members could view severe enforcement as unfair, which might lead to a negative backlash against the "unfair" franchisor.

In addition to facilitating the punishment of opportunistic behavior, network closure can facilitate the rewarding of honest and benevolent behavior. Both good and bad news travel more rapidly and extensively among a focal actor's trading partners in a dense network.

Closure and cooperative norms Because network closure increases feelings of identification and commonality with other actors, it also facilitates the emergence of group norms that serve as standards for appropriate behavior. Attempts to violate clear group norms can trigger stronger reactions among network members than attempts to violate unclear norms. Wuyts and Geyskens (2005) interviewed 177 purchasing managers at small and medium-sized firms about the governance of purchasing agreements with supplier firms. They find that detailed contracts are more effective governance mechanisms for reducing opportunism when the dyadic exchange relationship is more strongly embedded in a network of mutual contacts (i.e., when closure is high). Thus, the authors argue, in addition to fostering the reputational mechanism, closure fosters the emergence of norms regulating behavior and legitimating group sanctions in case of contract violations.

Closure and protection against exploitative brokering Closure can also mitigate information transfer problems associated with structural holes. When the vendor serves as go-between for otherwise unconnected firms, as in systems selling where the vendor bridges the structural hole between buyer and suppliers, the vendor firm might exploit this position and selectively pass on information from the upstream component suppliers to the downstream buyer firm. Buyers can avoid this information asymmetry by building ties directly with component suppliers, i.e., by increasing closure and reducing the structural holes in the information network (Wuyts et al. 2004).

Two-step leverage Triads may also assist actors in accessing and mobilizing resources indirectly through "two-step" leverage. In a study of an agro-business cooperative, Gargiulo (1993) examines a social network of 59 actors and finds that leaders built cooptive ties with actors who were in a position to affect their performance directly. When policy divergences or personal frictions made such ties untenable, leaders built strong ties with third parties able to influence those actors. Two-step leverage in an open triad may replace direct leverage in a dyad, as Gargiulo documents. However, two-step leverage can also be used in closed triads to further strengthen direct leverage in a dyad. For example, a customer who feels he is being treated unfairly by a car dealer can call upon the car manufacturer to exert influence on the car dealer. Also, vendors such as car dealers and systems integrators may try harder and treat their customers better if they know that periodic satisfaction surveys offer customers the opportunity to commend them to manufacturers.

The effectiveness of two-step leverage is largely contingent upon the third party's willingness and ability to exert influence. In a conjoint experiment, Wuyts and colleagues (2004) find that buyers have a stronger preference for system integrators with intensive ties to component suppliers if the buyers themselves have direct ties to component suppliers. Such preferences are consistent with two-step leverage: calling upon supplier firms to constrain a vendor is likely to be more effective if these supplier firms have intensive contacts with the buyer as well as the vendor.

Network Structure and Affective Commitment Although firm interactions may be mostly calculative, as Williamson (1996) posits, there are indications of affective dimensions as well (e.g., Kumar, Scheer, and Steenkamp 1995a, 1995b). The network structure in which channel participants are embedded will affect the degree to which they experience the economic or technical need to maintain a particular relationship; this is often referred to as their "calculative commitment" to these relationships (e.g., Geyskens et al. 1996). However, network structure may also impact channel members' "affective commitment," i.e., the extent to which they would like to maintain their relationship with specific partners, regardless of economic consequences. As we have discussed, strong ties and closure can increase feelings of identification with other actors, which in turn can lead to affective commitment. A case study of the New York City garment industry by Uzzi (1997) shows that actors embedded in personal and business networks sometimes decided to maintain ties with business partners even if that clearly deviated from maximizing their own economic interests in the short and long term.

Adverse Effects of Social Networks in Channel Coordination While social networks may contribute to channel coordination, one should not overlook potential adverse effects. As noted above, relational continuance can supersede economic imperatives in case of close social networks. Networks also create the possibility of multiple actors colluding against one other actor (Simmel 1950), leading to distrust that increases the level of opportunism. Moreover, exercising punishment power (through reputation, norm enforcement, or two-step leverage mechanisms) may intensify rather than alleviate inter-firm conflict (Lusch 1976), and consequently enhance opportunism in the dyad (John 1984). As discussed above, Antia and Frazier (2001) find that being centrally located or being part of a dense network constrained a firm from severely enforcing contracts, even in the presence of a contractual violation. However, as Wuyts and Geyskens (2005) point out, network closure may also reduce the incidence of such opportunistic contractual violations.

Accessing Resources Through Alliances

Firms ally with other firms primarily to gain access to external resources. Alliances enable firms to build critical mass to jointly fend off competition (often observed in the telecom and airline industries), access complementary technology for complex products (such as the cooperation between Apple, Sony, and Sharp for laptops), or access complementary marketing resources (such as alliances between pharmaceutical firms with a large sales force and biotech start-ups, or that between PepsiCo and Starbucks to commercialize the latter's DoubleShot and Frappuccino products). The alliance allows partners to identify available resources, but to realize the actual transfer of resources, the conditions of opportunity, motivation, and ability must be met. Below, we discuss how network structure can facilitate these conditions.

Identifying Network Resources In order to access external resources, one first needs to locate them. We have already discussed Granovetter's (1973) strength-of-weak-ties argument and noted that its key insight is about redundancy, not tie strength. We have also discussed the search-transfer problem, noting the benefits of bridging weak ties in locating new knowledge but their limitation in transferring that knowledge when it is complex rather than simple (Hansen 1999) or when it is very valuable (Frenzen and Nakamoto 1993).

A very interesting study by Rowley, Behrens, and Krackhardt (2000) investigates alliance networks in the steel-producing and semiconductor-manufacturing industries, and finds that a firm holding strong inter-firm ties performs better if the network of these ties is characterized by low density. This is consistent with the idea that, in the absence of network redundancy, strong ties are more valuable than weak ties. Interestingly, high closure among a firm's partners decreases performance in the semiconductor industry (where exploring new ideas is important) and increases performance in the steel industry (where exploiting existing ideas is important). This is consistent with the idea that the presence of bridging ties in the network boosts the search for new information, whereas network closure boosts the transfer and exploitation of knowledge.

Two other studies illustrate the importance of network nonredundancy for search and exploration. Wuyts, Dutta, and Stremersch (2004) examine alliance networks in the biopharmaceutical industry, where exploration is paramount, and find that firms with partners in diverse technological fields are more innovative than those with partners in overlapping technological fields. Rindfleisch and Moorman (2001) observe that tie strength and knowledge redundancy were inversely related in the alliance settings they studied. Horizontal alliances between competitors were characterized by low tie strength but high knowledge redundancy, whereas vertical alliances between channel members were characterized by high tie strength but low knowledge redundancy.

Accessing Network Resources Tie strength is a crucial explanatory variable in resource transfer. As discussed in Chapter 2, "tie strength" captures both the intensity and valence of interaction. Tie intensity (frequency of contact) determines the partners' ability to share resources. Valence is directly related to the motivation to share resources: if positive, both parties are more likely to be willing to exchange information. For instance, when firms in a learning alliance are also competing in markets beyond its scope, the alliance often fails since both firms try to leak as little knowledge as possible (Doz and Hamel 1998).

Tie strength is especially crucial for accessing knowledge that is complex (requiring higher ability for sharing to take place) and has proprietary value (requiring a higher motivation). Studies by Hansen (1999), Szulanski (1997), and Szulanski, Cappetta, and Jensen (2004) document how the understanding and absorption of more complex knowledge requires intensive interaction and relation-specific heuristics. A qualitative study at several Chicago-area banks (Uzzi and Lancaster 2003) finds that arm's-length ties were a popular means of accessing knowledge that was simple and publicly available, whereas the same ties inhibited effective transfer of private knowledge. Similarly, a study of franchised pizza restaurants finds that valuable procedural knowledge gained through learning-by-doing was shared with other units, but that the transfers were limited to units owned by the same franchisee (Darr, Argote, and Epple 1995).

The effects of closure and two-step leverage we discussed in the realm of channel coordination apply to alliances as well. Bae and Gargiulo (2004), for instance, analyze alliances in the U.S. telecommunications industry and find that a firm facing nonsubstitutable (and hence powerful) partners was better off when its alliances were embedded in third-party ties, which allowed the firm to gain indirect leverage in addition to direct leverage on such alliance partners.

Adverse Effects of Alliance Networks in Accessing External Resources The downside to using the network to access resources and knowledge transfer is knowledge leakage (Dutta and Weiss 1997). Networks that facilitate the assimilation of knowledge also enhance the risk of leaking strategically important knowledge to competitors since a firm's exchange partner may have ties with the focal firm's competitors. The exchange partner may also exploit its structural position in between the focal firm and its competitor, and collude with the competitor against the focal firm. Alternatively, the partner in the middle may play the focal firm and its competitor against each other (the *divide et impera* principle).

Gaining Status from One's Network

An important manifestation of the network as a resource is the perceived quality of a firm and its products (Podolny 1993, 2005; Stuart, Hoang, and Hybels 1999). Just as consumers use brand names to infer unobservable product quality, so do people and firms sometimes use a firm's network to make inferences about that firm and its products. This is called a status effect. Note that status is different from reputation: "Whereas reputation is a signal of quality and an indication of future behavior that is based largely on prior actions and behaviors, status is a signal of quality and an indication of future behavior that is based largely on the positions that occupants hold.…With status, there is an assumption that prior actions or achievements at some point led to one's position, but it is because of the positions themselves that occupants are accorded respect or not" (Smith 2005, p. 8). In practical terms, it is the difference between "I expect this firm will do well because it has performed well in the past" (reputation) and "I expect this firm will do well because it is connected to several prestigious firms" (status). Sometimes, the mere number of a firm's alliance partners can serve as a basis of quality and social status (Baker, Faulkner, and Fisher 1998).

A study of law firms in a large Midwestern city indicates that law firms with higher status, in the sense of belonging to a cluster of structurally equivalent law firms that serve more profitable clients, were able to negotiate higher prices (Uzzi and Lancaster 2004). This suggests that status derived from network position has dollar value. A study by Jensen (2003) of commercial banks' entry into investment banking between 1991 and 1997 finds that network status facilitated market entry. Also consistent with the interpretation that status is a proxy for unobserved quality, the effect decreased over time after market entry and network status was less important to customers with more market experience.

Managing Competition

Ties between competitors may not always be negative in valence. Managers of competing firms may form friendships. Cohesive friendship networks among competitors—characterized by strong ties, local closure, and overall density—can even lead to higher performance (Ingram and Roberts 2000). They do so by enhancing information exchange among firms and increasing collaboration, which may ultimately benefit customers, and also by mitigating competition, which in the extreme may result in tacit or explicit collusion.

Cohesive friendship networks may be especially important to maintaining collusion against customers who seek to play competitors against one another. Ingram and Roberts (2000) give examples from the Sydney hotel industry, where customers can negotiate lower prices by pitting one hotel against the other but where friendship networks among hotel managers contain the extent of competitive behavior. Density, however, also increases the chance of detection by investigators in truly collusive arrangements, as it is easier to be linked to other malfeasants. Baker and Faulkner (1993) find that centrally located managers in three price-fixing conspiracies had a higher chance of being found guilty and tended to receive stiffer sentences.

Multi-market contact among firms—which occurs when firms encounter the same rivals in many markets—may also soften competition (e.g., Gimeno and Woo 1999). It may strengthen oligopolistic coordination since the gains from aggressive competitive behavior in one market may be weighed against the danger of retaliatory forays by the competitor in other markets, especially in markets where the firm has more to lose. This suggests that suppliers with strongly overlapping segment or customer portfolios, i.e., with strong structural equivalence, may be able to better manage their rivalry than suppliers with lower levels of overlap and equivalence. This is somewhat at odds with the standard interpretation of equivalence as a metric of rivalry, and suggests the possibility of an inverse U-shaped relationship between structural equivalence and extent of competitive intensity between firms. However, we are not aware of any investigation into this conjecture. Moreover, contact over many markets also adds complexity, which may inhibit effective coordination (Evans and Kessides 1994). In short, the interrelationship between multi-market contact, structural equivalence, and the ability to manage competition is intriguing, but merely conjectural at this time.

Adopting New Suppliers, Technologies, and Practices

Our discussion of industrial buying behavior noted that members of decision-making units may use ties that cross firm boundaries to collect information. Here we discuss a few studies that explicitly study the role of inter-firm network ties in the context of adoption behavior.

Money, Gilly, and Graham (1998) examine how national culture affects referral behavior for industrial services such as advertising, banking, and accounting. Both U.S. and Japanese firms tended to rely more on strong ties outside their country of origin than in their own home market. This suggests that when uncertainty is higher, firms turn to stronger rather than weaker ties. This runs against a naïve interpretation of "the strength of weak ties" but is consistent with the more nuanced and accurate interpretation that strong ties are better at providing support and complex information.

An intriguing finding is that the referral networks that firms (either U.S. or Japanese) used outside their country of origin had more degree and betweenness centralization than those in their own home market. This might be because firms used central intermediaries to introduce them to others abroad, but also because firms chose to avoid closure in foreign countries out of fear of becoming overly dependent on a clique of densely interconnected alters. The data reported in the study do not allow one to adjudicate between these two possibilities.

In a study of 32 steel mills, Czepiel (1974, 1975) finds that they had regular opinion/advice relationships with on average two to three other firms in the industry. When considering the adoption of continuous casting as a new production method, steel mills contacted on average five to six other steel mills. Also, Czepiel finds that there were two cohesive subgroups. Members of the first subgroup consisted mostly of mini-mills and had several referral ties to the members of the other group consisting mostly of Big Steel firms, whereas only one tie went in the other direction. In other words, the network had the high status-low status structure described in our discussion of blockmodeling in Chapter 2. Interestingly, Czepiel finds no association between time of adoption and being an opinion leader (measured as number of nominations received, i.e., in-degree). So, the cautionary remark we made about not confusing being an influential consumer with being an early adopter translates to business markets as well.

A study of the diffusion of new technologies in the Australian insurance industry finds a very different network structure than Czepiel does in the U.S. steel industry. While the latter finds two densely interconnected subgroups with a high status-low status structure between them, Midgley, Morrison, and Roberts (1992) find a network without any subgroup. Instead, there were three firms centrally located in the network but with considerable overlap in their alters. The contrast between these two studies clearly indicates that it is hard to predict what network structure will occur in what industry unless one has at least some a priori knowledge about institutional details.

Finally, we draw attention to a branch of organizational theory called neo-institutionalism. This research tradition suggests that "technical" and "utilitarian-rational" mechanisms such as awareness, risk reduction, and competitive concerns are likely to operate early rather than late in the diffusion process, whereas the opposite is suggested for normative pressures. A study by Westphal, Gulati, and Shortell (1997) on the adoption of Total Quality Management (TQM) among 2,700 U.S. hospitals provides some support for this idea. They find that early adopters of TQM customized quality practices to the hospital's specific needs and capabilities, whereas late adopters were more likely to mimic TQM models adopted in other hospitals. Also, the mimetic behavior of late adopters was stronger for hospitals that had more ties to other hospitals that had already adopted TQM (pointing at conformity rather than economic efficiency as main motivation to adopt among late adopters). Not surprisingly, TQM provided significantly less economic benefits to late adopters. A study by Kraatz and Zajac (1996), however, finds little support for the hypothesis that technical considerations matter more early than late in the diffusion process. At this time, the conjecture must be treated as an interesting idea rather than as a documented fact.

7

Conclusions and Future Prospects

Summary Observations

There is ample evidence that the pattern of ties among people and among organizations matters. A few general themes emege from our review of research on networks among consumers, within firms, and among organizations. The most fundamental is the insight that closure or redundancy, on the one hand, hurts one's ability to find novel information but, on the other hand, helps to secure cooperation and access to the information and other resources one has located. A related insight is that strong ties help in mobilizing sources of support, and that weak ties are valuable only for information search and only to the extent that they exhibit less redundancy. A third insight is that network structure can have important effects on the spread of information, some of which are counterintuitive. Finally, network structure has consequences for many fundamental issues in human behavior and business, such as conflict and coordination, power, influence, change, and innovation. In spite of many interesting ideas and findings about social networks in general, and in business settings in particular, there still is a major gap between what marketers should know about social networks and the current stock of knowledge.

The large body of research on social contagion dynamics for new products was generated, in large part, before the emergence of the Internet and the Web. Very little is known about the salience and relevance of consumers' online ties. One would presume that many of these ties are weaker than offline ties, but also more numerous and spanning multiple communities of interests. How important are such online ties in generating awareness, sharing product information, and transferring attitudes about new and existing products? The answers are not clear.

We know especially little about how social network structure relates to the emergence and reproduction of communities of customers sharing strong brand beliefs and attitudes. How networks affect brand dynamics is an issue about which hardly anything is known.

Sociologists and management researchers have extensively studied how employees' social networks affect knowledge sharing within the organization. However, their focus has often been on technical knowledge, and little is known about the role of social networks in how market information disseminates within the firm or in how marketers learn about their markets. To the extent that market knowledge is simpler and more explicit than technical knowledge and deeply ingrained operational routines, informal networks may very well be less important for marketing. However, truly great marketers have intuitive understandings and insights based on deep engagement with the marketplace, which may not be easily shared except through face-to-face interaction. Moreover, market-oriented firms are characterized not only by the wide dissemination of information, but also by a strong culture. Personal interaction may be important in creating and sustaining such market-oriented cultures, but we cannot point to any specific evidence. In short, we have little or no direct evidence of how social networks help in sharing market knowledge and a market orientation throughout the organization.

Industrial buying is one of the few areas in marketing where the importance of social networks is not only considered "received wisdom" but is also supported by evidence. In particular, the relation between one's position in the decision-making unit (DMU) and one's influence and access to resources is well established. However, much of the evidence is several decades old, and extensive re-engineering of both firms and supply chains has occurred over the last 15 years.

As to inter-organizational contexts, the gap between current and desired knowledge is quite large as well. With regard to channel coordination, several empirical studies in fields outside of marketing have pointed to the importance of network governance, yet little evidence exists as to the precise network mechanisms at play and their relative influence within marketing channels. With regard to alliance networks, the large body of research in the areas of strategy and organization focuses on technological rather than marketing alliances, and transferring and managing technology may be different from transferring market knowledge and managing marketing activities. Another key issue about which very little is known, in marketing as well as in other disciplines, is how and why organizational networks form and evolve over time.

So, as much as we believe that network research provides valuable conceptual tools and empirical insights, quite a bit of work remains to be done. Below, we discuss a number of research challenges and opportunities. Research is motivated by problems and requires bringing together theory to frame problems, data to have some indication of what is actually going on, and analytical tools providing valid and meaningful insights by linking theory and data (Lilien 1994; Merton 1968). We see several challenges and opportunities to further our knowledge of social networks in marketing. In our discussion, we note a fairly large number of substantive research issues, but also draw attention to some issues pertaining to data and analytical tools.

Substantive Problems and Challenges

Word-of-Mouth Marketing There is now a sizable body of theoretical propositions and empirical regularities on word-of-mouth and social influence. Future research efforts should assess the effectiveness of word-of-mouth and similar viral campaigns. How much is gained from identifying and leveraging opinion leaders using social network data that are often hard and, hence, expensive to collect as compared to using cheaper attribute data? In pharmaceuticals, for instance, opinion leaders tend to be high prescribers. Since prescription data are easy to obtain, it is important to know whether costly network analysis adds much value. Here, as in other areas, marketing practice can learn a lot from controlled experiments or even quasi-experiments (e.g., Gensch, Aversa, and Moore 1990; Lilien et al. 2002; Lodish et al. 1995a, 1995b; Riskey 1997). One can envision controlled field experiments, where one set of sales reps focuses on their usual prospects, another set focuses on opinion leaders profiled using a larger set of attributes, and a third set focuses on opinion leaders and those they are connected to profiled through network analysis. However, such experiments are easier to conduct when the marketing consists of direct mail rather than personal selling. For a recent example, see the study by Hill, Provost, and Volinsky (2006) of a campaign by AT&T.

A challenge in using word-of-mouth marketing is scalability. For many products, the cost of collecting network data in each important city or community one seeks to target would be prohibitive. Over time, marketers could build a model based on more readily available attribute and affiliation data from which to predict network structure among target customers. It is unclear whether such a model could make its "network structure predictions" sufficiently informative to identify likely opinion leaders and guide micro-targeting decisions. Only experience will tell, but visionary marketers willing to go through the learning exercise may end up with a tool that boosts their marketing ROI.

Organizational Buying Behavior Like word-of-mouth, this is an area with some well-established ideas. However, the way supplier and buyer companies interact has changed dramatically over the last 20 years, and marketing theory may well be out of touch with how buying decisions are typically being made today and how the actors involved typically relate to each other. For example, since firms have become much more interconnected over the last 20 years, ties to other buyer firms, suppliers, or channel partners may be much more important in organizational buying behavior today than the bulk of existing research and frameworks suggests.

Gaining and Sharing Market Information Among the most fundamental marketing beliefs is that firms benefit from being market oriented and that the marketing function plays a prominent role in connecting with the customer (e.g., Jaworski and Kohli 1993; Moorman and Rust 1999). A social network perspective can presumably further our understanding of how the marketing function is (or should be) networked, both externally with customers and internally with other functions, to optimally gather, process, and disseminate market information. Similarly, account managers, who occupy brokerage positions between the customer and the firm, need to manage their relationship with the customer while also assuring access to the expertise and knowledge of their colleagues within the firm to provide optimal customer solutions. Again, a social network approach may lead to interesting insights that can help explain why some account managers perform better than others. Finally, as network positions are clearly associated with power, our discipline may benefit from investigating how the influence of the marketing function and the acceptance of market orientation within the firm are associated with the social network position of marketers within their firm.

Brands and Brand Communities There is an increasing interest among marketing practitioners and branding experts in sociological and cultural issues such as how brand identities come to exist and evolve through social practices (e.g., the importance of the European rave scene early in Red Bull's history), and how brand cultures engage or disengage from general culture (e.g., Holt 2004). Brand communities are another phenomenon of great interest to marketers where brands, culture, and social interaction come into play (e.g., Atkin 2004; Kozinets 2002; Muniz and O'Guinn 2001; Ragas and Bueno 2002). Unfortunately, the literature on social networks in market settings does not provide much insight on these issues. It tends to ignore the meaning of ties and the relation between social network structure and cognitive structures (Smith-Doerr and Powell 2005). At a high level of abstraction, the relation between network analysis and cultural analysis is problematic (Emirbayer and Goodwin 1994; Nadel 1957), but there is some research that clearly relates network structure and culture and that might serve as a source of inspiration to enterprising marketing scholars (Martin 2002; McLean 1998). There also are other streams of research offering some more concrete ideas and findings to build on.

First, the current literature on consumer and brand culture counts several contributions that clearly connect to macroscopic social structure (e.g., Holt 1997, 1998; Kozinets and Handelman 2004), and at least one gets close to social network issues conceptually though not operationally (Muniz and O'Guinn 2001). Second, research on recruitment in social movements has long investigated social networks and is now also paying more attention to powerful symbols and cultural frames (e.g., Jasper and Poulsen 1995; McAdam and Paulsen 1993; Snow, Zurcher, and Ekland-Olson 1980). Third, there is some work on relating social and cognitive structures by Carley (1986) that has attracted considerable attention in the sociology of knowledge and which might have relevance to brands as well. Finally, another advance may come from reversing the question. Rather than asking what networks can do for brand communities, marketers should also ask what their brand communities can do for their customers' networks. It is long accepted that consumers use consumption as a means to building and maintaining a social position (Bourdieu 1984; Douglas and Isherwood 1979; Holt 1998; Molnár and Lamont 2002). Can brand communities act in the same way? They can, if consumers treat attitudes towards the brand and other brand-related cognitions as "accounting systems [used] in deciding whether particular relations are worth starting up or maintaining" (DiMaggio 1992, p. 119). The same holds for brand cultures. To the extent that brand communities and brand cultures can serve customers as accounting systems and sorting devices in their social networks (e.g., using brand community membership to infer who they would like to socialize with), they will have a reason to maintain a strong involvement with the brand.

Marketing Channels Social network analysis seems a "natural fit" for channels research and can be used to investigate brokerage, competition, and coordination issues that go beyond the dyadic level. The competition of two manufacturers vying for the support of the same reseller who fills a structural hole towards consumers is rather obvious. A network perspective also highlights coordination issues. For instance, the quality of work and customer satisfaction of a systems integrator may well be enhanced if two key suppliers cooperate with each other, but that same cooperation amounts to closure which may diminish the systems integrator's ability to appropriate a large part of the value created. So, network structure may shed a new and more intense light on issues of brokerage, competition, and coordination pertaining to two key issues in business strategy: value creation and value appropriation. Based on prior theory and research, we expect that even relatively small extensions from channel dyads to very small networks with three to five actors may be enough to learn about such complex issues.

Another type of research, more fundamental and focusing on network structure itself rather than on its consequences, would be to collect data on actual distribution systems and to study the structure of ties (Wilkinson 1976). Are there some types of positions that keep occurring, and if so, with what frequency (e.g., Bonacich and Bienenstock 1997; Marsden 1989)? Are there particular "motifs" or subnetwork structures that keep occurring, as Milo et al. (2002) find for networks in biochemistry, neurobiology, ecology, and engineering? Is there a systematic association between the frequency of positions or motifs and the country, industry, or product category? Answers to these descriptive questions might raise new analytical questions, which in turn may help to sharpen our understanding of distribution channels.

New Product Development Firms are increasingly looking beyond their formal boundaries for addressing the challenge of generating customer-relevant innovations (e.g., Baum, Calabrese, and Silverman 2000). Approaches are plentiful, such as involving consultants or product development firms (Hargadon and Sutton 1997), listening in to dialogues between customers and virtual advisors (Urban and Hauser 2004), or allying with complementary or competing firms (Sivadas and Dwyer 2000). With so many opportunities to access external knowledge for superior new product development, one would like to know what kinds of positions in what kinds of networks with what kind of external partners are most beneficial.

Resource-based View of the Firm Social networks can provide access to information and other resources. But business theory tells us that sticky resources are the key to a sustainable competitive advantage. So, what is the role of inter-organizational networks in how firms sustain competitive advantages? Do they help firms to continuously renew their portfolio of resources and manage conditions of dynamic misfit created by stretch goals (Itami 1987)? Do they allow firms to combine strong commitment to core resources with a sufficient level of flexibility (Ghemawat 1991)? Or does the advantage lie in the processes and activities that firms deploy within their own boundaries and within their dyadic ties to create value by combining the resources accessed externally with resources already present internally, as Håkansson (1987) suggests? The latter perspective puts greater emphasis on the role of activities than most social network research we covered in this volume, which focused on actors, the resources they control, and the structure of the ties among the actors. To make network theory more valuable to managers, the structural approach we emphasized may have to be complemented with a better understanding of what actually happens within the ties.

Getting Good Data

Data Accuracy and Measurement Unlike most other types of research, network analysis requires information not only about discrete entities but also about connections between those entities. Some connections are easy to observe, like proximity ties based on physical distance. Others leave a trace that is easy to capture. In organizational networks, for example, official and other records capture capital investments in ventures, R&D alliances, and, in some cases, commercial transactions. In personal networks, capturing connections is more difficult. Some ties may be traceable from secondary sources, like kin relations and people's affiliation to the same organization, such as the hospital they work at or the university and year of graduation. Some ties are recorded automatically, especially those taking place through electronic media, like email. However, many other types of personal con-

nections can be measured only through surveys which may be onerous to adminis-
ter and tend to suffer from imperfect accuracy stemming from poor memory
(Brewer 2000), differences across respondents' interpretations of questions
(Bearman and Parigi 2004), and even self-report biases, as when respondents think
they have many friends or have access to powerful others (Feld and Carter 2002).
Over the years, analysts have developed tools and procedures that limit these problems (Marsden 1990, 2005). Better research is likely to come from using better measurement instruments, and the value of network research in marketing is likely to
depend on it.

Cost Since collecting primary network data in large populations through surveys
can be quite onerous and expensive, some researchers will try other ways of collecting data.

One way is to "piggyback" on already existing data. For instance, researchers
investigating intra-organizational networks may have access to electronically
recorded data on telephone and email interaction or on visits to company intranet
sites acting as "live" document-sharing devices or as repositories of technical documents. To investigate consumer networks, researchers may use links between blogs,
"friendships" in social networking sites like LinkedIn, or "trusted reviewer" links in
peer product review sites like Epinions. In studies of organizational networks, many
studies have used patent citations and overlaps in the board of directors. In all these
cases, one must ask whether these data reflect meaningful ties relevant for one's
research problem. If not, researchers will not be very different from drunks looking
for their lost keys under lamp posts because that's where the light is.

Another approach to collecting data is to use physical proximity as a proxy for
social proximity and, thus, social influence. There are several problems with this
approach. First, physical distance is only one driver of communication between
two actors (e.g., Van den Bulte and Moenaert 1998). Second, spatial proximity may
lead to only a coarse differentiation among actors. Let's take ZIP codes as an example. Approximating the social network by ZIP code membership implies that all
actors within the same ZIP code are structurally equivalent. That is, each person or
household has the same pattern of ties with all other actors in their own ZIP code
and with all other actors in each other's ZIP code. Whether the loss of information
induced by this coarseness is worth the costs savings is an empirical question. One
might expect that such a proxy would be more useful in a large population of
undifferentiated consumers than in (1) consumer markets with opinion leaders or
(2) business markets and professional markets where a small number of accounts
can generate a large proportion of total sales. Finally, and most problematically,
people and firms tend to co-locate with similar others. For instance, income and
wealth determine to a large degree one's neighborhood. In the United States, where

the quality of the public schools varies dramatically across districts, people with children may have a tendency to prefer a particular location because of school quality, whereas singles and empty-nesters would not. The outcome of this self-selection process is that spatial proximity correlates highly with similarity in attributes. Proximity and attribute profile may be highly correlated even in the absence of self-selection. National culture and income per capita, for instance, tend to be more similar across nearby, rather than across distant, countries. Unless these attributes are controlled for in the analysis, similarity in behavior across proximate actors cannot be interpreted as evidence of social influence.

A third approach to efficiently study networks is to use experiments rather than field data. One can create "artificial worlds" with varying network structures and investigate how these differences affect people's behavior. As consumer researchers have long understood, experiments often have the benefit of being cheap and, when well designed, allow one to draw strong causal inferences about what affects what. Conjoint experiments, for instance, are a methodology that is long accepted in both marketing academia and business and that can easily be applied to networks as well (e.g., Wuyts et al. 2004).

Analytical Tools

Increasing the Level of Expertise among Marketing Researchers   Marketing researchers often apply theories from economics or psychology and are typically trained in applied statistics. Since none of those disciplines pays much attention to networks, marketing lacks theoretical-substantive and technical-analytical knowledge and skills about social networks. This is not likely to change as long as structural sociology and social anthropology continue to be omitted from the formal education of future marketers at the undergraduate, M.B.A., and Ph.D. levels. If industry creates sufficient demand pull for marketing researchers trained in network theory and analysis, educational institutions would follow. In the meantime, however, firms will lack expertise not only in their managerial ranks but also among the traditional vendors of market research.

Networks and Game Theory   Much of the interest of financiers, managers, and business scholars in social networks lies in how networks affect conflict, competition, cooperation, coordination, and value appropriation. Each of those issues is also studied, in very rigorous mathematical terms, by applied game theorists who, however, have tended to ignore network structure. That is in sharp contrast to social network analysis in economic sociology and strategic management, where networks are central but the theorizing often remains purely verbal.[22] In biology and sociology a large body of literature uses computer simulations to investigate game-theoretical issues, and especially cooperation, in network structures (e.g., Abramson and Kuperman 2001; Macy and Willer 2002; Ohtsuki et al. 2006). One intriguing result from one of those simulation studies is the following. Watts and Strogatz (1998) report that in Iterated Prisoners' Dilemma games where players have to choose between cooperation and defection, the well-known "tit-for-tat" strategy—that in two-player games favors the emergence of the optimal all-cooperate outcome—was less likely to achieve this outcome in a "small world" with high-local-clustering-yet-short-average-geodesic than in a so-called "regular lattice" where the local clustering is lower but the average geodesic is longer. One would expect the lower local clustering to make punishment after defection less effective, but we wonder to what extent the presence of "short-cut ties" linking otherwise very remote parts of the network may expose actors to different parts of the network where possibly different strategies are being deployed. Sticking to tit-for-tat may be more difficult when facing a greater variety of strategies. If research would show the latter intuition to be correct, then it would imply a drawback of bridging ties and a caveat to the standard strength-of-weak-ties argument.

Network Change and Evolution Networks change over time as the result of "natural tendencies" like structural balance, external random events, and interventions like a merger of firms or the introduction of project-based teams. Researchers investigating network change (e.g., Newcomb 1961) have faced two challenges: data and proper statistical models. Data are likely to become more available, especially for electronically mediated communication. Statistical models are also becoming less of a stumbling block with the development of new methods, some of which are easy to use (Hoff, Raftery, and Handcock 2002; Iacobucci and Wasserman 1988; Robins and Pattison 2001; Snijders 2001; van Duijn, Busschbach, and Snijders 1999).

A much greater challenge is the mutual dependency between network structure and actor's behavior (or "agency" as social theorists call it). Structure affects actors' behaviors and outcomes; realizing this, actors will take steps to change their position in the structure. Hence, structure and behavior are both "dependent variables." This circularity or mutual endogeneity creates major problems statistically and theoretically (Emirbayer 1997; Emirbayer and Goodwin 1994; Fuchs 2001; Robins and Pattison 2005). To our knowledge, sociologists and statisticians are still far from resolving these problems. While marketers should be wary of purposeful behavior when studying network evolution and of endogeneity when studying network effects, we do not believe that it is marketing researchers' role to resolve the structure-agency problem or to build new statistical models that encompass both structure and behavior or outcomes as dependent variables. They have much more immediate and soluble problems to apply themselves to.

Glossary

Actor	Node in a social network
Adjacency matrix	Matrix in which each row i and each column j represents a node or actor and the $(i,j)^{th}$ cell represents the tie from i to j
Alter	An actor to whom a focal actor is connected; a neighbor to the focal actor in an egocentric network
Betweenness centrality	Number of times that a focal actor occurs on the shortest path or geodesic between all pairs of actors in a network
Blockmodeling	Method of reorganizing an adjacency matrix to identify subgroups of actors that are structurally equivalent
Clique	Subgroup of actors that contains at least three actors who are all connected to each other, and that is not contained in another clique
Closeness centrality	The average geodesic distance between a focal actor and all other actors in the network
Closure	The density among those with whom one has a tie
Degree centrality	Number of direct ties an actor has
Density	The proportion of possible ties in a network that are actually present
Directionality	A tie between A and B is directional when it is specified that it flows from A to B, or from B to A, or both.

Dyad	A pair of nodes and the (possible) tie(s) between them
Ego	The focal actor in an egocentric network
Egocentric network	The network consisting of an actor (ego) and the actors he or she is connected to (alters or neighbors), as well as the ties among all these actors
Geodesic	Shortest path (in terms of number of steps) between two actors in a network
Homophily	Tendency for actors to connect with other actors who are similar rather than dissimilar to them
In-degree	Number of an actor's incoming ties
k-*plex*	A subgroup containing n nodes, in which all actors are directly connected to at least $n - k$ other members of the subgroup
k-*core*	A subgroup in which all actors have direct ties with at least k other actors in the subgroup.
Multiplexity	The presence of multiple kinds of ties between two actors
n-*clique*	Subgroup of actors that contains at least three actors, all of whom are connected by a shortest path of length n or less (i.e., either directly or through a maximum of $n - 1$ intermediates), and with the additional requirement that no other actor in the network has a shortest path distance of n or less to each and all members of the n-clique
Neighbor	Node to which another node is connected through a tie
Node	Discrete entity in a network; often graphically represented as a point connected (or not) through lines to other points
Out-degree	Number of an actor's outgoing ties
Reciprocity	A tie between A and B is reciprocal if it is bi-directional, i.e., if the tie is directed and symmetric (a flow occurs from A to B and from B to A).

Social capital	Those aspects of social structure that can be used by actors to realize their interests
Social contagion	Phenomenon that actors are influenced in their behavior through exposure to other actors' knowledge, attitude, or behavior. Imitation is the most common form of social contagion.
Social network	A set of discrete social entities and the collection of ties between them
Social tie	Link between a pair of social entities
Sociogram	Graphical representation of the social network, with actors as points or nodes and ties as lines connecting them
Sociocentric network	A network the nodes of which are not selected based on their being connected to a focal node; the label "sociocentric" is useful only as a contrast to "egocentric"
Structural balance	A set of actors is structurally balanced when any two actors sharing a positive tie are consistent in their evaluation of all other actors and when any two actors sharing a negative tie are inconsistent in their evaluation of all other actors.
Structural equivalence	Similarity between two actors in terms of commonality of contacts
Structural equivalence matrix	Matrix in which the $(i,j)^{th}$ cell contains a metric of structural equivalence between the actor of row i and the one of column j
Structural hole	If a tie that uniquely connects two parts of the network that, without it, would be unconnected, actors involved in such a tie are said to "fill" or "bridge" a structural hole.
Structural isomorphism	Similarity between two actors in terms of the structure of their portfolios of ties (not necessarily involving the same contacts)

Symmetry	A tie between A and B is symmetric if it is bi-directional, i.e., if the tie is directed and flows from A to B as well as from B to A; a symmetric tie is also called reciprocal.
Tie	Link or connection between two nodes in a network
Tie strength	Combination of tie intensity/activity (in terms of frequency of contact) and tie valence (in terms of the affective, supportive, or cooperative character of the tie)
Transitivity	A relation is transitive if the presence of a tie between A and B and between B and C also implies the presence of a tie between A and C.
Two-step leverage	(1) Reducing dependency on a neighboring actor by building ties to other actors that can exert influence on that actor; (2) accessing resources through an indirect path with one intermediary rather than through a direct tie

Appendix: Suggestions for Further Reading

Nontechnical popular science

Here are two "popular science" books on networks in general but with many examples pertaining to social networks.

Mark Buchanan (2002), *Nexus: Small Worlds and the Groundbreaking Theory of Networks.* New York, N.Y.: W. W. Norton & Company.

Duncan J. Watts (2003), *Six Degrees: The Science of a Connected Age.* New York, N.Y.: W. W. Norton & Company.

On social network analysis

This list of six books is ranked in order of complexity. The first four books can serve for self-study or as course textbooks. They range from introductory to intermediate. The book by de Nooy, Mrvar, and Batagelj is especially recommended to those looking for a hands-on approach combining conceptual exposition with hands-on application of techniques with computer software. The last two books are advanced and quite technical.

Alain Degenne and Michel Forsé (1999), *Introducing Social Networks.* London, U.K.: Sage Publications.

John P. Scott (2000), *Social Network Analysis: A Handbook*, 2nd ed. London, U.K.: Sage Publications.

Wouter de Nooy, Andrej Mrvar, and Vladimir Batagelj (2005), *Exploratory Social Network Analysis with Pajek.* Cambridge, U.K.: Cambridge University Press.

Peter J. Carrington, John Scott, and Stanley Wasserman, eds. (2005), *Models and Methods in Social Network Analysis.* Cambridge, U.K.: Cambridge University Press.

Stanley Wasserman and Katherine Faust (1994), *Social Network Analysis: Methods and Applications.* Cambridge, U.K.: Cambridge University Press.

Mark Newman, Albert-László Barabási, and Duncan J. Watts, eds. (2006), *The Structure and Dynamics of Networks.* Princeton, N.J.: Princeton University Press.

On word-of-mouth

These four books are ranked in order of rigor, but all are rather easy reading. Silverman is a consultant who uses some outlandish hyperbole at times but also offers some very interesting insights. Rosen is a former high-tech marketer with a more disciplined style of thinking and writing. His book is easy to read, but carefully thought out. Rogers is a key source on how word-of-mouth affects the uptake of new products, and Weimann offers a thorough overview of academic research on opinion leadership until the early 1990s.

George Silverman (2001), *The Secrets of Word-of-Mouth Marketing: How to Trigger Exponential Sales Through Runaway Word of Mouth*. New York, N.Y.: AMACOM.

Emanuel Rosen (2000), *The Anatomy of Buzz: How to Create Word of Mouth Marketing*. New York, N.Y.: Doubleday.

Everett M. Rogers (2003), *Diffusion of Innovations*, 5th ed. New York, N.Y.: Free Press.

Gabriel Weimann (1994), *The Influentials: People Who Influence People*. Albany, N.Y.: State University of New York Press.

On intra- and inter-organizational networks

The book by Cross and Parker is targeted towards managers and consultants. Burt combines theory and empirical research and presents important new insights, in a style that is accessible to interested nonspecialists. Kilduff and Tsai's book is a succinct textbook, which can also be read for self-study. The final volume is a collection of papers illustrating several uses of network analysis.

Robert L. Cross and Andrew Parker (2004), *The Hidden Power of Social Networks: Understanding How Work Really Gets Done in Organizations*. Boston, Mass.: Harvard Business School Press.

Ronald Burt (1992), *Structural Holes: The Social Structure of Competition*. Cambridge, Mass.: Harvard University Press.

Martin Kilduff and Wenpin Tsai (2003), *Social Networks and Organizations*. London, U.K.: Sage Publications.

Nitin Nohria and Robert G. Eccles, eds. (1992), *Networks and Organizations: Structure, Form, and Action*. Boston, Mass.: Harvard Business School Press.

Beyond technical tools and business settings

These four books are suggested for those seeking to learn about a broader body of theory and research. Leinhardt presents a collection of 24 classic papers in social network research in anthropology, sociology, and social psychology. The book saves one many trips to the library and allows one to read about the ideas in the original. Wasserman and Galaskiewicz present a handy collection of review papers covering applications of social network analysis in various disciplines, from management to anthropology to epidemiology. Lin focuses on the benefits of networks, but does not limit his scope to business settings. Swedberg's book is limited to economic settings, but covers many issues and concepts beyond networks.

Samuel Leinhardt, ed. (1977), *Social Networks: A Developing Paradigm*. New York, N.Y.: Academic Press.

Stanley Wasserman and Joseph Galaskiewicz, eds. (1994), *Advances in Social Network Analysis: Research in the Social and Behavioral Sciences*. Thousand Oaks, Calif.: Sage Publications.

Nan Lin (2001), *Social Capital: A Theory of Social Structure and Action*. Cambridge, U.K.: Cambridge University Press.

Richard Swedberg (2003), *Principles of Economic Sociology*. Princeton, N.J.: Princeton University Press.

Resources on the Web

The home page of the International Network for Social Network Analysis (INSNA) is: http://www.insna.org/

This webpage is a great resource. It lists tutorials, courses on social network analysis being taught, descriptions of software packages, links to several prominent researchers' websites, and several other valuable bits of information. Also, since it is the website of a noncommercial, not-for-profit organization of researchers, one does not have to worry about mercantile biases.

The Word of Mouth Marketing Association (WOMMA) is a trade association for the word-of-mouth marketing industry. Its website posts some interesting materials: http://womma.org/

Notes

1. Though some very interesting research has been done on those "marginal" areas (Biggart 1989; Coughlan and Grayson 1998; Frenzen and Davis 1990), it is of interest mostly to academics seeking to assess and extend the boundaries of traditional theorizing.

2. Even though Russian banks ended up applying several of the key ideas in social network theory, we doubt that they developed these solutions from such theory. It is more likely that the banks had already absorbed several of the key ideas from experience. The idea of "peer monitoring," for instance, has a very long history in commercial finance (e.g., Greif 1993) and had already been discussed in the economics literature by 1990 (Arnott and Stiglitz 1990; Stiglitz 1990).

3. In some extreme cases, network effects might conceivably result in the entire market being locked into an inferior product that just happened to have an early lead. The odds of such lock-in by an inferior technology, however, may be much lower than commonly believed: the popular examples of QWERTY keyboards and Betamax VCRs do not stand up to scrutiny (Liebowitz and Margolis 1990, 1994, 1999)

4. The top journals in marketing (*Journal of Consumer Research, Journal of Marketing, Journal of Marketing Research,* and *Marketing Science*) publish network-type research only rarely. Moreover, some of the articles that have appeared in these journals contain theoretical mistakes, like misrepresenting the strength-of-weak-tie argument. Another bit of evidence, anecdotal but telling, is how the editor of a top marketing journal once rejected a social network-based paper because, so he claimed, all results were already well known in sociology, after which the paper— revised but presenting the same data and results—was submitted and rather swiftly accepted for publication by the editors of the *American Journal of Sociology* at the University of Chicago.

5. That is not to say that the latter research is not quite valuable. Two "popular science" books provide a friendly introduction, and provide many examples of how

the ideas pertain to social networks as well: Buchanan (2002) and Watts (2003). For a more academic but not overly technical review, see Watts (2004). For more thorough and complete discussions, see review papers by Albert and Barabási (2002) and Newman (2003) or the book volume edited by Newman, Barabási, and Watts (2006) presenting a collection of the most influential papers.

6. Some specialists prefer to define a relation as the collection of all ties of a specific kind among a specific set of actors (Wasserman and Faust 1994). For instance, "friendship" is a relation and "is a friend of" is a tie that exists between actors in a network. The distinction is important in mathematics and in some specific parts of network theory, but will rarely be critical for our purpose here.

7. Things change, though, when one uses multiple attributes such that groups can overlap and an actor can be a member of multiple groups at the same time. We discuss such a scenario later on, under the label "cross-cutting social circles." Note also that when groups overlap, one can define a network with groups as nodes and the extent of overlap as ties, and analyze that network of groups using standard network methods.

8. Distinguishing between these two dimensions of tie strength has an interesting parallel with a separation of two components in group solidarity, another area where researchers have long struggled with ideas of strength. Several have now proposed to partition the notion of solidarity into a relational component, the observed connections among actors, and an ideational component referring to the actors' identification with their collective (Doreian and Fararo 1998; Moody and White 2003; Mudrack 1989). Note that the former component refers to overt behavior, while the latter refers to a more cognitive and affective dimension.

9. Students of consumer psychology will recognize that structural balance is akin to Heider's concept of cognitive balance that itself is the basis of much of attitudinal theory relevant to consumer behavior, marketing communication, and branding.

10. For networks of n actors with directional ties, each actor can send a tie to each of the n - 1 other actors, so the total possible number of ties is $n \times (n-1)$. If the ties are nondirectional, one must divide that number by 2 to avoid double counting.

11. Closure is also identical to what Watts and Strogatz (1998) call "clustering," but the latter term is lately being used to refer to something else, the mean probability that two actors connected to a common third actor will be connected to each other, i.e., the tendency for transitivity at the level of the entire network (Newman, Barabási, and Watts 2006, pp. 286–8).

12. From a mathematical point of view, this "recursive" idea raises a problem of infinite regress. It happens that it can be resolved by expressing the network in terms of a matrix and then computing the "eigenvector" corresponding to the largest "eigenvalue" of the matrix. Hence the name "eigenvector centrality."

13. The behavior oriented towards expectations is often referred to as a "social role" in general sociological and anthropological theory (e.g., Linton 1936; Merton 1968). However, social network analysts often use the same term to refer to a pure "formal" or "graph-theoretical" concept of associations among relations that link social positions (Wasserman and Faust 1994, p. 349). We find the notion of role in social network analysis, including how it relates to other notions like position, to be very complex and so have decided not to discuss it in this primer. Nadel (1957) provides a key theoretical discussion, of which DiMaggio (1992) distills the essence. Borgatti and Everett (1992) provide a very useful discussion of structural equivalence and structural isomorphism that also covers their connection to social roles.

14. Several other problems exist with this study that are bound to have biased the result in favor of the "small world" finding. For instance, 100 of the 196 participants living in Nebraska were blue chip stockowners, and were hence much more likely to have a short path to a stock broker near Boston than any source randomly chosen from the U.S. population. See Kleinfeld (2002).

15. Both definitions are similar in spirit to an earlier one by Bourdieu (1980) presenting social capital as the actual or potential resources that stem from having a durable network of more or less institutionalized relationships of mutual acquaintance or recognition. As Portes (1998, p. 1) points out, Bourdieu's definition of social capital "makes clear that social capital is decomposable into two elements: first, the social relationship itself that allows individuals to claim access to resources possessed by their associates and second, the amount and quality of those resources."

16. Some may prefer to label such indirect endogenous feedback mediated through suppliers' decisions "ecological influence" rather than "social contagion," to distinguish it from more direct interpersonal or inter-organizational influence (Marsden and Friedkin 1994).

17. The rule assumes that the firm has enough resources to support one seeding point per dense subgroup. If that is not the case, then the firm will want to add a third criterion favoring actors with more bridging ties to other dense subgroups. Otherwise, it may end up with one actor per cluster but not necessarily the one that has bridging ties to outsiders.

18. The evidence of leader-leader and seeker-seeker interaction in the opinion leadership literature is consistent with the more recent evidence, mentioned in Chapter 2, that social networks tend to exhibit homophily or "assortative mixing" by degree, where people with more (fewer) ties tend to be connected with other people who, like them, have more (fewer) ties (Newman 2002; Newman and Park 2003).

19. Of course, if opinion leaders tend to have exacting standards which a product cannot meet, then the firm might be better off avoiding the leaders. In a study about the trial of a new coffee, Arndt (1967) finds that receivers of unfavorable word-of-mouth were 24% less likely to buy the new product than those not receiving any word-of-mouth, whereas those receiving favorable word-of-mouth were 12% more likely to buy than the baseline group. So, in that study, negative word-of-mouth had about twice the effect of positive word-of-mouth.

20. A more recent study by Burt (2004) investigates this directly and presents evidence that managers spanning structural holes and hence having fewer redundant ties are more likely to express ideas, less likely to have ideas dismissed, and more likely to have ideas evaluated as valuable. This is consistent with the strength of weak tie and structural holes arguments. However, it is not quite clear whether Burt's findings are due to these managers having genuinely better ideas or simply to their having more power within their organization. Another study by Cross and Cummings (2004) of the association between betweenness centrality and subjective performance ratings of 101 engineers in a petrochemical company and 125 consultants in a strategy-consulting firm suffers from a similar problem. The findings are suggestive but not conclusive, since the way that project managers rate the performance of project participants may exhibit a bias correlated with the participants' centrality.

21. The reputational mechanism probably also becomes increasingly effective over time as reputations develop. Consistent with this idea, Larson (1992) finds in a qualitative study of seven highly cooperative interfirm alliances in four industries, that the preservation of organizational reputations became gradually intertwined with economic exchange, strengthening the reputational control mechanism as exchange relationships matured.

22. Some exceptions that do use game theoretical analysis include Bienenstock and Bonacich (1997), Bonacich and Bienenstock (1993, 1995), Buskens (1998, 2003), Buskens and Weesie (2000), Raub and Weesie (1990), Greif (1993, 1994), Greif, Milgrom, and Weingast (1994), and Montgomery (1996, 1998).

References

Abramson, Guillermo, and Marcelo Kuperman (2001), "Social Games in a Social Network." *Physical Review E* 63, 030901.

Achrol, Ravi S., and Philip Kotler (1999), "Marketing in the Network Economy." *Journal of Marketing* 63 (Special Issue), 146–63.

Alba, Richard D., and Charles Kadushin (1976), "The Intersection of Social Circles: A New Measure of Social Proximity in Networks." *Sociological Methods and Research* 5 (1), 77–102.

Albert, Réka, and Albert-László Barabási (2002), "Statistical Mechanics of Complex Networks." *Reviews of Modern Physics* 74 (1), 47–97.

Allen, Thomas J. (1977), *Managing the Flow of Technology: Technology Transfer and the Dissemination of Technological Information within the R&D Organization.* Cambridge, Mass.: MIT Press.

Amaral, L. A. N., A. Scala, M. Barthélémy, and H. E. Stanley (2000), "Classes of Small-World Networks." *Proceedings of the National Academy of Sciences of the United States of America* 97 (21), 11149–52.

Antia, Kersi, and Gary L. Frazier (2001), "The Severity of Contract Enforcement in Interfirm Channel Relationships." *Journal of Marketing* 65 (4), 67–81.

Arndt, Johan (1967), "Role of Product-Related Conversations in the Diffusion of a New Product." *Journal of Marketing Research* 4 (3), 291–5.

Arndt, Johan (1979), "Toward a Concept of Domesticated Markets." *Journal of Marketing* 43 (4), 69–75.

Arndt, Johan (1983), "The Political Economy Paradigm: Foundation for Theory Building in Marketing." *Journal of Marketing* 47 (4), 44–54.

Arnott, Richard, and Joseph E. Stiglitz (1990), "Moral Hazard and Nonmarket Institutions: Dysfunctional Crowding Out or Peer Monitoring." *American Economic Review* 81 (1), 179–90.

Atkin, Douglas (2004), *The Culting of Brands: When Customers Become True Believers.* New York, N.Y.: Portfolio.

Axelrod, Robert (1984), *The Evolution of Cooperation.* New York, N.Y.: Basic Books.

Bae, Jonghoon, and Martin Gargiulo (2004), "Partner Substitutability, Alliance Network Structure, and Firm Profitability in the Telecommunications Industry." *Academy of Management Journal* 47 (6), 843–59.

Baker, Wayne E. (1994), *Networking Smart: How to Build Relationships for Personal and Organizational Success*. New York, N.Y.: McGraw-Hill.

Baker, Wayne E. (2000), *Achieving Success through Social Capital: Tapping the Hidden Resources in Your Personal and Business Networks*. San Francisco, Calif.: Jossey-Bass.

Baker, Wayne E., and Robert R. Faulkner (1993), "The Social Organization of Conspiracy: Illegal Networks in the Heavy Electrical Equipment Industry." *American Sociological Review* 58 (6), 837–60.

Baker, Wayne E., Robert R. Faulkner, and Gene A. Fisher (1998), "Hazards of the Market: The Continuity and Dissolution of Interorganizational Market Relationships." *American Sociological Review* 63 (2), 147–77.

Balkundi, Prasad, and David A. Harrison (2006), "Ties, Leaders, and Time in Teams: Strong Inference about Network Structure's Effects on Team Viability and Performance." *Academy of Management Journal* 49 (1), 49–68.

Ball, Frank, Denis Mollison, and Gianpaolo Scalia-Tomba (1997), "Epidemics with Two Levels of Mixing." *Annals of Applied Probability* 7 (1), 46–89.

Ball, Sheryl, Catherine Eckel, Philip J. Grossman, and William Zame (2001), "Status in Markets." *Quarterly Journal of Economics* 116 (1), 161–88.

Balter, David, and John Butman (2005), *Grapevine: The New Art of Word-of-Mouth Marketing*. New York, N.Y.: Portfolio.

Bandura, Albert (1986), *Social Foundations of Thought and Action: A Social Cognitive Theory*. Englewood Cliffs, N.J.: Prentice-Hall.

Baum, Joel A.C., Tony Calabrese, and Brian Silverman (2000), "Don't Go It Alone: Alliance Network Composition and Start-ups' Performance in Canadian Biotechnology." *Strategic Management Journal* 21 (3), 267–94.

Baum, Joel A.C., Andrew V. Shipilov, and Tim J. Rowley (2003), "Where Do Small Worlds Come From?" *Industrial & Corporate Change* 12 (4), 697–725.

Baumgarten, Steven A. (1975), "The Innovative Communicator in the Diffusion Process." *Journal of Marketing Research* 12 (1), 12–8.

Bearden, William O., and Michael J. Etzel (1982), "Reference Group Influence on Product and Brand Purchase Decisions." *Journal of Consumer Research* 9 (2), 183–94.

Bearden, William O., Richard G. Netemeyer, and Jesse E. Teel (1989), "Measurement of Consumer Susceptibility to Interpersonal Influence." *Journal of Consumer Research* 15 (4), 473–81.

Bearman, Peter, and Paolo Parigi (2004), "Cloning Headless Frogs and Other Important Matters: Conversation Topics and Network Structure." *Social Forces* 83 (2), 535–57.

Becker, Marshall H. (1970), "Sociometric Location and Innovativeness: Reformulation and Extension of the Diffusion Model." *American Sociological Review* 35, 267–83.

Beckman, Christine M., and Damon J. Phillips (2005), "Interorganizational Determinants of Promotion: Client Leadership and the Attainment of Women Attorneys." *American Sociological Review* 70 (4), 678–701.

Bemmaor, Albert C. (1994), "Modeling the Diffusion of New Durable Goods: Word-of-Mouth Effect versus Consumer Heterogeneity." In *Research Traditions in Marketing*, eds. Gilles Laurent, Gary L. Lilien, and Bernard Pras, 201–23. Boston, Mass.: Kluwer Academic Publishers.

Berger, Jonah, and Chip Heath (2007), "Where Consumers Diverge From Others: Identity-Signaling and Product Domains." *Journal of Consumer Research* 34 (2), in press.

Berner, Robert (2006), "I Sold It through the Grapevine." *Business Week* 3986 (May 29), 32–4.

Bian, Yanjie (1997), "Bringing Strong Ties Back In: Indirect Ties, Network Bridges, and Job Searches in China." *American Sociological Review* 62 (3), 366–85.

Bienenstock, Elisa Jayne, and Phillip Bonacich (1997), "Network Exchange as a Cooperative Game." *Rationality & Society* 9 (1), 37–65.

Biggart, Nicole Woolsey (1989), *Charismatic Capitalism: Direct Selling Organizations in America*. Chicago, Ill.: University of Chicago Press.

Blau, Peter M. (1955), *The Dynamics of Bureaucracy: A Study of Interpersonal Relations in Two Government Agencies*. Chicago, Ill.: University of Chicago Press.

Blau, Peter M. (1977), *Inequality and Heterogeneity: A Primitive Theory of Social Structure*. New York, N.Y.: Free Press.

Boissevain, Jeremy (1974), *Friends of Friends: Networks, Manipulators, and Coalitions*. Oxford, U.K.: Blackwell.

Bonacich, Phillip, and Elisa Jayne Bienenstock (1993), "Assignment Games, Chromatic Number, and Exchange Theory." *Journal of Mathematical Sociology* 17 (4), 243–59.

Bonacich, Phillip, and Elisa Jayne Bienenstock (1995), "When Rationality Fails: Unstable Exchange Networks With Empty Cores." *Rationality & Society* 7 (3), 293–320.

Bonacich, Phillip, and Elisa Jayne Bienenstock (1997), "Latent Classes in Exchange Networks: Sets of Positions with Common Interest." *Journal of Mathematical Sociology* 22 (1), 1–28.

Bond, Edward U., III, Beth A. Walker, Michael D. Hutt, and Peter H. Reingen (2004), "Reputational Effectiveness in Cross-Functional Working Relationships." *Journal of Product Innovation Management* 21 (1), 44–60.

Bonus, Holger (1973), "Quasi-Engel Curves, Diffusion, and the Ownership of Major Consumer Durables." *Journal of Political Economy* 81, 655–77.

Borgatti, Stephen P., and Martin G. Everett (1992), "Notions of Position in Social Network Analysis." *Sociological Methodology* 22, 1–35.

Bourdieu, Pierre (1980), "Le Capital Social: Notes Provisoires." *Actes de la Recherche en Sciences Sociales* 31, 2–3.

Bourdieu, Pierre (1984), *Distinction: A Social Critique of the Judgment of Taste.* Cambridge, Mass.: Harvard University Press.

Brass, Daniel J., Joseph Galaskiewicz, Henrich R. Greve, and Wenpin Tsai (2004), "Taking Stock of Networks and Organizations: A Multilevel Perspective." *Academy of Management Journal* 47 (6), 795–817.

Brewer, Devon D. (2000), "Forgetting in the Recall-Based Elicitation of Personal and Social Networks." *Social Networks* 22 (1), 29–43.

Brin, Sergey, and Lawrence Page (1998), "The Anatomy of a Large-Scale Hypertextual Web Search Engine." *Computer Networks and ISDN Systems* 30 (1-7), 107–17.

Bristor, Julia M. (1993), "Influence Strategies in Organizational Buying: The Importance of Connections to the Right People in the Right Places." *Journal of Business-to-Business Marketing* 1 (1), 63–98.

Bristor, Julia M., and Michael J. Ryan (1987), "The Buying Center Is Dead, Long Live the Buying Center." *Advances in Consumer Research* 14, 255–8.

Brown, Jacqueline Johnson, and Peter H. Reingen (1987), "Social Ties and Word-of-Mouth Referral Behavior." *Journal of Consumer Research* 14 (3), 350–62.

Brown, John Seely, and Paul Duguid (1991), "Organizational Learning and Communities-of-Practice: Toward a Unified View of Working, Learning, and Innovation." *Organization Science* 2 (1), 40–57.

Brown, John Seely, and Paul Duguid (2001), "Knowledge and Organization: A Social-Practice Perspective." *Organization Science* 12 (2), 198–213.

Brown, Lawrence A. (1981), *Innovation Diffusion: A New Perspective.* New York, N.Y.: Methuen.

Buchanan, Mark (2002), *Nexus: Small Worlds and the Groundbreaking Theory of Networks.* New York, N.Y.: W.W. Norton.

Burkhardt, Marlene E., and Daniel J. Brass (1992), "Changing Patterns or Patterns of Change: The Effects of a Change in Technology on Social Network Structure and Power." *Administrative Science Quarterly* 35 (1), 104–27.

Burnkrant, Robert E., and Alain Counsineau (1975), "Informational and Normative Social Influence in Buyer Behavior." *Journal of Consumer Research* 2 (3), 206–15.

Burt, Ronald S. (1987), "Social Contagion and Innovation: Cohesion versus Structural Equivalence." *American Journal of Sociology* 92 (6), 1287–335.

Burt, Ronald S. (1990), "Kinds of Relations in American Discussion Networks." In *Structures of Power and Constraint: Papers in Honor of Peter M. Blau,* eds. Craig Calhoun, Marshall W. Meyer, and W. Richard Scott, 411–51. Cambridge, U.K.: Cambridge University Press.

Burt, Ronald S. (1992), *Structural Holes: The Social Structure of Competition.* Cambridge, Mass.: Harvard University Press.

Burt, Ronald S. (1997), "A Note on Social Capital and Network Content." *Social Networks* 19 (4), 355–73.

Burt, Ronald S. (1998), "The Gender of Social Capital." *Rationality & Society* 10 (1), 5–46.

Burt, Ronald S. (1999), "Entrepreneurs' Distrust and Third Parties: A Strategic Look at the Dark Side of Dense Networks." In *Shared Cognition in Organizations*, eds. Leigh L. Thompson, John M. Levine, and David M. Messick, 213–43. Mahwah N.J.: Lawrence Erlbaum Associates.

Burt, Ronald S. (2004), "Structural Holes and Good Ideas." *American Journal of Sociology* 110 (2), 349–99.

Buskens, Vincent (1998), "The Social Structure of Trust." *Social Networks* 20 (3), 265–89.

Buskens, Vincent (2003), "Trust in Triads: Effects of Exit Control and Learning." *Games & Economic Behavior* 42 (2), 235–52.

Buskens, Vincent, and Jeroen Weesie (2000), "Cooperation via Social Networks." *Analyse & Kritik* 22 (1), 44–74.

Calder, Bobby J. (1977), "Structural Role Analysis in Organizational Buying: A Preliminary Investigation." In *Consumer and Industrial Buying Behavior*, eds. Arch G. Woodside, Jagdish N. Sheth, and Peter D. Bennett, 193–200. New York, N.Y.: North Holland.

Carley, Kathleen (1986), "An Approach for Relating Social Structure to Cognitive Structure." *Journal of Mathematical Sociology* 12 (2), 137–89.

Castilla, Emilio J. (2005), "Social Networks and Employee Performance in a Call Center." *American Journal of Sociology* 110 (5), 1243–83.

Chatterjee, Rabikar, and Jehoshua Eliashberg (1990), "The Innovation Diffusion Process in a Heterogeneous Population: A Micromodeling Approach." *Management Science* 36, 1057–79.

Childers, Terry L., and Akshay R. Rao (1992), "The Influence of Familial and Peer-based Reference Groups on Consumer Decisions," *Journal of Consumer Research* 19 (2), 198–211.

Coleman, James S. (1988), "Social Capital in the Creation of Human Capital." *American Journal of Sociology* 94 (Supplement), S95–S120.

Coleman, James S. (1990), *Foundations of Social Theory*. Cambridge, Mass.: Harvard University Press.

Coleman, James S., Elihu Katz, and Herbert Menzel (1966), *Medical Innovation: A Diffusion Study*. Indianapolis, Ind.: The Bobbs-Merrill Company.

Cook, K.S., and J.M. Whitmeyer (1992), "Two Approaches to Social Structure: Exchange Theory and Network Analysis." *Annual Review of Sociology* 18, 109–27.

Coughlan, Anne T., and Kent Grayson (1998), "Network Marketing Organizations: Compensation Plans, Retail Network Growth, and Profitability." *International Journal of Research in Marketing* 15 (5), 401–26.

Coulter, Robin A., Lawrence Feick, and Linda L. Price (2002), "Changing Faces: Cosmetics Opinion Leadership among Women in the New Hungary." *European Journal of Marketing* 36, 1287–308.

Cross, Rob, and Jonathan N. Cummings (2004), "Tie and Network Correlates of Individual Performance in Knowledge-Intensive Work." *Academy of Management Journal* 47 (6), 928–37.

Cross, Robert L., and Andrew Parker (2004), *The Hidden Power of Social Networks: Understanding How Work Really Gets Done in Organizations.* Boston, Mass.: Harvard Business School Press.

Cyert, Richard M., Herbert A. Simon, and Donald B. Trow (1956), "Observation of a Business Decision." *Journal of Business* 29, 237–48.

Czepiel, John A. (1974), "Word-of-Mouth Processes in the Diffusion of a Major Technological Innovation." *Journal of Marketing Research* 11 (2), 172–80.

Czepiel, John A. (1975), "Patterns of Interorganizational Communications and the Diffusion of a Major Technological Innovation in a Competitive Industrial Community." *Academy of Management Journal* 18 (1), 6–24.

Dalton, Melville (1955), *Men Who Manage: Fusions of Feeling and Theory in Administration.* New York, N.Y.: John Wiley.

Darr, Eric D., Linda Argote, and Dennis Epple (1995), "The Acquisition, Transfer, and Depreciation of Knowledge in Service Organizations: Productivity in Franchises." *Management Science* 41 (11), 1750–62.

Davis, Fred D., Richard P. Bagozzi, and Paul R. Warshaw (1989), "User Acceptance of Computer Technology: A Comparison of Two Theoretical Models." *Management Science* 35, 982–1003.

Davis, Gerald F., Mina Yoo, and Wayne E. Baker (2003), "The Small World of the American Corporate Elite 1982-2001." *Strategic Organization* 1 (3), 301–26.

Davis, James A. (1970), "Clustering and Hierarchy in Interpersonal Relations: Testing Two Graph Theoretical Models on 742 Sociomatrices." *American Sociological Review* 35 (5), 843–51.

Davis, James A. (1977), "Sociometric Triads as Multi-Variate Systems." *Journal of Mathematical Sociology* 5 (1), 41–59.

Dawes, Philip L., and Don Y. Lee (1996), "Communication Intensity in Large-Scale Organizational High Technology Purchasing Decisions." *Journal of Business-to-Business Marketing* 3 (3), 3–38.

Dawes, Philip L., Don Y. Lee, and Grahame R. Dowling (1998), "Information Control and Influence in Emergent Buying Centers." *Journal of Marketing* 62 (3), 55–69.

Day, George S., and Robin Wensley (1983), "Marketing Theory with a Strategic Orientation." *Journal of Marketing* 47 (4), 79–89.

Delacroix, Jacques, and Hayagreeva Rao (1994), "Externalities and Ecological Theory: Unbundling Density Dependence." In *Evolutionary Dynamics of Organizations*, eds. Joel A.C. Baum and Jitendra V. Singh, 255–68. New York, N.Y.: Oxford University Press.

Deutsch, Morton, and Harold B. Gerard (1955), "A Study of Normative and Information Social Influences upon Individual Judgment." *Journal of Abnormal and Social Psychology* 51, 629–36.

DiMaggio, Paul (1992), "Nadel's Paradox Revisited: Relational and Cultural Aspects of Organizational Culture." In *Networks and Organizations: Structure, Form, and Action*, eds. Nitin Nohria and Robert G. Eccles, 118–42. Boston, Mass.: Harvard Business School Press.

DiMaggio, Paul, and Hugh Louch (1998), "Socially Embedded Consumer Transactions: For What Kinds of Purchases Do People Most Often Use Networks?" *American Sociological Review* 63 (5), 619–37.

DiMaggio, Paul J., and Walter W. Powell (1983), "The Iron Cage Revisited: Institutional Isomorphism and Collective Rationality in Organizational Fields." *American Sociological Review* 48, 147–60.

Dodds, Peter Sheridan, Roby Muhamad, and Duncan J. Watts (2003), "An Experimental Study of Search in Global Social Networks." *Science* 301, 827–9.

Dollinger, Marc J., Peggy A. Golden, and Todd Saxton (1997), "The Effect of Reputation on the Decision to Joint Venture." *Strategic Management Journal* 18 (2), 127–40.

Doreian, Patrick, and Thomas Fararo (1998), *The Problem of Solidarity: Theories and Models*. Amsterdam, The Netherlands: Gordon & Breach.

Douglas, Mary, and Baron Isherwood (1979), *The World of Goods*. New York, N.Y.: Basic Books.

Doz, Yves L., and Gary Hamel (1998), *Alliance Advantage—The Art of Creating Value Through Partnering*. Boston, Mass.: Harvard Business School Press.

Dutta, Shantanu, and Allen M. Weiss (1997), "The Relationship between a Firm's Level of Technological Innovativeness and Its Patterns of Partnership Agreements." *Management Science* 43 (3), 343–56.

Dyer, Jeffrey H., and Harbir Singh (1998), "The Relational View: Cooperative Strategy and Sources of Interorganizational Competitive Advantage." *Academy of Management Review* 23 (4), 660–79.

Eccles, Robert G., and Dwight B. Crane (1988), *Doing Deals: Investment Banks at Work*. Boston, Mass.: Harvard Business School Press.

Emerson, Richard M. (1962), "Power-Dependence Relations." *American Sociological Review* 27 (1), 31–41.

Emirbayer, Mustafa (1997), "Manifesto for a Relational Sociology." *American Journal of Sociology* 103 (2), 281–317.

Emirbayer, Mustafa, and Jeff Goodwin (1994), "Network Analysis Culture and the Problem of Agency." *American Journal of Sociology* 99 (6), 1411–54.

Evans, William N., and Ioannis N. Kessides (1994), "'Living by the "Golden Rule': Multimarket Contact in the U.S. Airline Industry." *Quarterly Journal of Economics* 109 (2), 341–66.

Feld, Scott L. (1997), "Structural Embeddedness and Stability of Interpersonal Relations." *Social Networks* 19 (1), 91–5.

Feld, Scott L., and William C. Carter (2002), "Detecting Measurement Bias in Respondent Reports of Personal Networks." *Social Networks* 24 (4), 365–83.

Fernandez, Roberto M., Emilio J. Castilla, and Paul Moore (2000), "Social Capital at Work: Networks and Employment at a Phone Center." *American Journal of Sociology* 105 (5), 1288–356.

Flynn, Leisa Reinecke, Ronald E. Goldsmith, and Jacqueline K. Eastman (1996), "Opinion Leaders and Opinion Seekers: Two New Measurement Scales." *Journal of the Academy of Marketing Science* 24 (2), 137–47.

Fortunato, Santo, Vito Latora, and Massimo Marchiori (2004), "Method to Find Community Structures Based on Information Centrality." *Physical Review E* 70, 056104.

Franklin, Benjamin (2005), *The Autobiography of Benjamin Franklin: Penn Reading Project Edition*. Philadelphia, Penn.: University of Pennsylvania Press.

Frenzen, Jonathan K., and Harry L. Davis (1990), "Purchasing Behavior in Embedded Markets." *Journal of Consumer Research* 17 (1), 1–12.

Frenzen, Jonathan K., and Kent Nakamoto (1993), "Structure, Cooperation, and the Flow of Market Information." *Journal of Consumer Research* 20 (3), 360–75.

Friestad, Marian, and Peter Wright (1994), "The Persuasion Knowledge Model: How People Cope with Persuasion Attempts." *Journal of Consumer Research* 21 (1), 1–31.

Friestad, Marian, and Peter Wright (1995), "Persuasion Knowledge: Lay People's and Researchers' Beliefs about the Psychology of Advertising." *Journal of Consumer Research* 22 (1), 62–74.

Fuchs, Stephan (2001), "Beyond Agency." *Sociological Theory* 19 (1), 24–40.

Fukuyama, Francis (1995), *Trust: The Social Virtues and the Creation of Prosperity*. New York, N.Y.: Free Press.

Gargiulo, Martin (1993), "Two-Step Leverage: Managing Constraint in Organizational Politics." *Administrative Science Quarterly* 38 (1), 1–19.

Gensch, Dennis H., Nicola Aversa, and Steven P. Moore (1990), "A Choice-Modeling Market Information System That Enabled ABB Electric to Expand Its Market Share." *Interfaces* 20 (1), 6–25.

Gerlach, Michael L. (1992), *Alliance Capitalism: The Social Organization of Japanese Business*. Berkeley, Calif.: University of California Press.

Geyskens, Inge, Jan-Benedict E.M. Steenkamp, Lisa K. Scheer, and Nirmalya Kumar (1996), "The Effects of Trust and Interdependence on Relationship Commitment: A Trans-Atlantic Study." *International Journal of Research in Marketing* 13 (4), 303–17.

Ghemawat, Pankaj (1991), *Commitment: The Dynamic of Strategy*. New York, N.Y.: Free Press.

Gimeno, Javier, and Carolyn Y. Woo (1999), "Multimarket Contact Economies of Scope and Firm Performance." *Academy of Management Journal* 42 (3), 239–59.

Girvan, M., and M. E. J. Newman (2002), "Community Structure in Social and Biological Networks." *Proceedings of the National Academy of Sciences of the United States of America* 99 (12), 7821–6.

Gladwell, Malcolm (2000), *The Tipping Point: How Little Things Can Make a Big Difference*. Boston, Mass.: Little Brown.

Gouldner, Alvin (1960), "The Norm of Reciprocity: A Preliminary Statement." *American Sociological Review* 25 (2), 161–78.

Granovetter, Mark (1973), "The Strength of Weak Ties." *American Journal of Sociology* 78 (6), 1360–80.

Granovetter, Mark S. (1978), "Threshold Models of Collective Action." *American Journal of Sociology* 83, 1420–43.

Granovetter, Mark S. (1982), "The Strength of Weak Ties: A Network Theory Revisited." In *Social Structure and Network Analysis*, eds. Peter V. Marsden and Nan Lin, 105–30. Beverly Hills, Calif.: Sage Publications.

Granovetter, Mark S. (1992), "Problems of Explanation in Economic Sociology." In *Networks and Organizations: Structure, Form, and Action*, eds. Nitin Nohria and Robert G. Eccles, 25–56. Boston, Mass.: Harvard Business School Press.

Granovetter, Mark (1995), *Getting a Job: A Study of Contacts and Careers*, 2nd ed. Chicago, Ill.: University of Chicago Press.

Greif, Avner (1993), "Contract Enforceability and Economic Institutions in Early Trade: The Maghribi Traders' Coalition." *American Economic Review* 83 (3), 525–48.

Greif, Avner (1994), "Cultural Beliefs and the Organization of Society: A Historical and Theoretical Reflection on Collectivist and Individualist Societies." *Journal of Political Economy* 102 (5), 912–50.

Greif, Avner, Paul Milgrom, and Barry R. Weingast (1994), "Coordination, Commitment, and Enforcement: The Case of the Merchant Guild." *Journal of Political Economy* 102 (4), 745–76.

Griffin, Abbie, and John R. Hauser (1992), "Patterns of Communication among Marketing Engineering and Manufacturing—A Comparison between Two New Product Teams." *Management Science* 38 (3), 360–73.

Griffin, Abbie, and John R. Hauser (1996), "Integrating R&D and Marketing: A Review and Analysis of the Literature." *Journal of Product Innovation Management* 13 (3), 191–215.

Grönroos, Christian (1994), "From Marketing Mix to Relationship Marketing: Towards a Paradigm Shift in Marketing." *Management Decision* 32 (2), 4–20.

Grover, Roland (2006), "The Pornographers vs. the Pirates." *BusinessWeek* 3989 (June 19), 68–9.

Guseva, Alya (2005), "Building New Markets: A Comparison of the Russian and American Credit Card Markets." *Socio-Economic Review* 3 (3), 437–66.

Guseva, Alya, and Akos Rona-Tas (2001), "Uncertainty, Risk, and Trust: Russian and American Credit Card Markets Compared." *American Sociological Review* 66 (5), 623–46.

Håkansson, Håkan (1982), *International Marketing and Purchasing of Industrial Goods: An Interaction Approach.* Chichester, U.K.: Wiley.

Håkansson, Håkan, ed. (1987), *Industrial Technological Development: A Network Approach.* London, U.K.: Croom Helm.

Håkansson, Håkan, and Ivan Snehota (1989), "No Business Is an Island: The Network Concept of Business Strategy." *Scandinavian Journal of Management* 5 (3), 187–200.

Hannan, Timothy H., and John M. McDowell (1987), "Rival Precedence and the Dynamics of Technology Adoption: An Empirical Analysis." *Economica* 54, 155–71.

Hansen, Morten T. (1999), "The Search-Transfer Problem: The Role of Weak Ties in Sharing Knowledge Across Organizational Subunits." *Administrative Science Quarterly* 44 (1), 81–111.

Hargadon, Andrew (2003), *How Breakthroughs Happen—The Surprising Truth About How Companies Innovate.* Boston, Mass.: Harvard Business School Press.

Hargadon, Andrew, and Robert I. Sutton (1997), "Technology Brokering and Innovation in a Product Development Firm." *Administrative Science Quarterly* 42 (4), 716–49.

Henderson, Geraldine R., Dawn Iacobucci, and Bobby J. Calder (1998), "Brand Diagnostics: Mapping Branding Effects Using Consumer Associative Networks." *European Journal of Operational Research* 111 (2), 306–27.

Henderson, Geraldine R., Dawn Iacobucci, and Bobby J. Calder (2002), "Using Network Analysis to Understand Brands." *Advances in Consumer Research* 29 (1), 397–405.

Hill, Shawndra, Foster Provost, and Chris Volinsky (2006), "Network-Based Marketing: Identifying Likely Adopters via Consumer Networks." *Statistical Science* 21 (2), 256–76.

Hoff, Peter D., Adrian E. Raftery, and Mark S. Handcock (2002) "Latent Space Approaches to Social Network Analysis." *Journal of the American Statistical Association* 97, 1090–98.

Holland, Paul W., and Samuel Leinhardt (1972), "Some Evidence on the Transitivity of Positive Interpersonal Sentiment." *American Journal of Sociology* 77 (6), 1205–9.

Holt, Douglas B. (1997), "Poststructuralist Lifestyle Analysis: Conceptualizing the Social Patterning of Consumption in Postmodernity." *Journal of Consumer Research* 23 (4), 326–50.

Holt, Douglas B. (1998), "Does Cultural Capital Structure American Consumption?" *Journal of Consumer Research* 25 (1), 1–25.

Holt, Douglas B. (2004), *How Brands Become Icons: The Principles of Cultural Branding.* Boston, Mass.: Harvard Business School Press.

Houston, Mark, Michael Hutt, Christine Moorman, Peter H. Reingen, Aric Rindfleisch, Vanitha Swaminathan, and Beth Walker (2004), "A Network Perspective on Marketing Strategy Performance." In *Assessing Marketing Strategy Performance,* eds. Christine Moorman and Donald R. Lehmann, 247–68. Boston, Mass.: Marketing Science Institute.

Houston, Mark B., and Shane A. Johnson (2000), "Buyer-Supplier Contracts versus Joint Ventures: Determinants and Consequences of Transaction Structure." *Journal of Marketing Research* 37 (1), 1–15.

Hughes, Mark (2005), *Buzzmarketing: Get People to Talk about Your Stuff.* New York, N.Y.: Portfolio.

Huisman, Mark, and Marijtje A.J. van Duijn (2005), "Software for Social Network Analysis." In *Models and Methods in Social Network Analysis,* eds. Peter J. Carrington, John Scott, and Stanley Wasserman, 270–316. Cambridge, U.K.: Cambridge University Press.

Hutt, Michael D., Peter H. Reingen, and John R. Ronchetto, Jr. (1988), "Tracing Emergent Processes in Marketing Strategy Formation." *Journal of Marketing* 52 (1), 4–20.

Iacobucci, Dawn, ed. (1996), *Networks in Marketing.* Thousand Oaks, Calif.: Sage Publications.

Iacobucci, Dawn, and Jonathan D. Hibbard (1999), "Toward an Encompassing Theory of Business Marketing Relationships (BMRs) and Interpersonal Commercial Relationships (ICRs): An Empirical Generalization." *Journal of Interactive Marketing* 13 (3), 13–33.

Iacobucci, Dawn, and Nigel Hopkins (1992), "Modeling Dyadic Interactions and Networks in Marketing." *Journal of Marketing Research* 26 (1), 5–17.

Iacobucci, Dawn, and Amy Ostrom (1996), "Commercial and Interpersonal Relationships: Using the Structure of Interpersonal Relationships to Understand Individual-to-Individual, Individual-to-Firm, and Firm-to-Firm Relationships in Commerce." *International Journal of Research in Marketing* 13 (1), 53–72.

Iacobucci, Dawn, and Stanley Wasserman (1988), "A General Framework for the Statistical Analysis of Sequential Dyadic Interaction Data." *Psychological Bulletin* 103, 379–90.

Ibarra, Herminia (1992), "Homophily and Differential Returns: Sex Differences in Network Structure and Access in an Advertising Firm." *Administrative Science Quarterly* 37 (3), 422–47.

Ibarra, Herminia (1995), "Race, Opportunity, and Diversity of Social Circles in Managerial Networks." *Academy of Management Journal* 38 (3), 673–703.

Ingram, Paul, and Peter W. Roberts (2000), "Friendships among Competitors in the Sydney Hotel Industry." *American Journal of Sociology* 106 (2), 387–424.

Itami, Hiroyuki (1987), *Mobilizing Invisible Assets*. Cambridge, Mass.: Harvard University Press.

Jasper, James M., and Jane D. Poulsen (1995), "Recruiting Strangers and Friends: Moral Shocks and Social Networks in Animal Rights and Anti-Nuclear Protests." *Social Problems* 42 (4), 493–512.

Jaworski, Bernard, and Ajay K. Kohli (1993), "Market Orientation: Antecedents and Consequences." *Journal of Marketing* 57 (3), 53–71.

Jensen, Michael (2003), "The Role of Network Resources in Market Entry: Commercial Banks' Entry into Investment Banking 1991-1997." *Administrative Science Quarterly* 48 (3), 466–97.

Johanson, Jan, and Lars-Gunnar Mattsson (1994), "The Markets-as-Networks Tradition in Sweden." In *Research Traditions in Marketing,* eds. Gilles Laurent, Gary L. Lilien, and Bernard Pras, 321–42. Boston, Mass.: Kluwer.

John, George (1984), "An Empirical Investigation of Some Antecedents of Opportunism in a Marketing Channel." *Journal of Marketing Research* 21 (3), 278–89.

Johnston, Wesley J., and Thomas V. Bonoma (1981), "The Buying Center: Structure and Interaction Patterns." *Journal of Marketing* 45 (3), 143–56.

Kadushin, Charles (1966), "The Friends and Supporters of Psychotherapy: On Social Circles in Urban Life." *American Sociological Review* 31 (6), 786–802.

Katz, Elihu, and Paul F. Lazarsfeld (1955), *Personal Influence: The Part Played by People in the Flow of Mass Communications.* New York, N.Y.: Free Press.

Katz, Michael L., and Carl Shapiro (1994), "Systems Competition and Network Effects." *Journal of Economic Perspectives* 8, 93–115.

Keeling, M.J. (1999), "The Effect of Local Spatial Structure on Epidemiological Invasions." *Proceedings of the Royal Society of London B*, 266, 859-67.

Keller, Ed, and Jon Berry (2003), *The Influentials: One American in Ten Tells the Other Nine How to Vote, Where to Eat, and What to Buy.* New York, N.Y.: Free Press.

Keller, Kevin Lane (2002), *Branding and Brand Equity.* Cambridge, Mass.: Marketing Science Institute.

Kilduff, Martin, and David Krackhardt (1994), "Bringing the Individual Back in: A Structural Analysis of the Internal Market for Reputation in Organizations." *Academy of Management Journal* 37 (1), 87–108.

King, Charles W., and John O. Summers (1970), "Overlap of Opinion Leadership across Consumer Product Categories." *Journal of Marketing Research* 7 (1), 43–50.

Kirzner, Israel M. (1973), *Competition and Entrepreneurship*. Chicago, Ill.: University of Chicago Press.

Kirzner, Israel M. (1979), *Perception, Opportunity, and Profit: Studies in the Theory of Entrepreneurship*. Chicago, Ill.: University of Chicago Press.

Kleinfeld, Judith S. (2002), "The Small World Problem." *Society* 39 (2), 61–6.

Kogut, Bruce, and Gordon Walker (2001), "The Small World of Germany and the Durability of National Networks." *American Sociological Review* 66 (3), 317–35.

Korte, Charles, and Stanley Milgram (1970), "Acquaintance Networks between Racial Groups: Application of the Small World Method." *Journal of Personality and Social Psychology* 15 (2), 101–8.

Kozinets, Robert V. (2002), "The Field Behind the Screen: Using Netnography for Marketing Research in Online Communities." *Journal of Marketing Research* 39 (1), 61–72.

Kozinets, Robert V., and Jay M. Handelman (2004), "Adversaries of Consumption: Consumer Movements, Activism, and Ideology." *Journal of Consumer Research* 31 (3), 691–704.

Kraatz, Matthew S., and Edward J. Zajac (1996), "Exploring the Limits of the New Institutionalism: The Causes and Consequences of Illegitimate Organizational Change." *American Sociological Review* 61 (5), 812–36.

Krackhardt, David (1990), "Assessing the Political Landscape: Structure, Cognition, and Power in Organizations." *Administrative Science Quarterly* 35 (2), 342–69.

Krackhardt, David (1992), "The Strength of Strong Ties: The Importance of Philos in Organizations." In *Networks and Organizations: Structure, Form, and Action*, eds. Nitin Nohria and Robert G. Eccles, 216–39. Boston, Mass.: Harvard Business School Press.

Krackhardt, David (1996), "Structural Leverage in Marketing." In *Networks in Marketing*, ed. Dawn Iacobucci, 50–9. Thousand Oaks, Calif.: Sage.

Krackhardt, David, and Daniel J. Brass (1994), "Intra-Organizational Networks: The Micro Side." In *Advances in Social Network Analysis: Research in the Social and Behavioral Sciences*, eds. Stanley Wasserman and Joseph Galaskiewicz, 207–29. Thousand Oaks, Calif.: Sage Publications.

Krackhardt, David, and Jeffrey R. Hanson (1993), "Informal Networks: The Company behind the Charts." *Harvard Business Review* 71 (4), 104–11.

Krackhardt, David, and Lyman W. Porter (1985), "When Friends Leave: A Structural Analysis of the Relationship between Turnover and Stayers' Attitudes." *Administrative Science Quarterly* 30 (2), 242–61.

Krackhardt, David, and Lyman W. Porter (1986), "The Snowball Effect: Turnover Embedded in Communication Networks." *Journal of Applied Psychology* 71 (1), 50–5.

Kumar, Nirmalya, Lisa K. Scheer, and Jan-Benedict E.M. Steenkamp (1995a), "The Effects of Supplier Fairness on Vulnerable Resellers." *Journal of Marketing Research* 32 (1), 54–65.

Kumar, Nirmalya, Lisa K. Scheer, and Jan-Benedict E.M. Steenkamp (1995b), "The Effect of Perceived Interdependence on Dealer Attitudes." *Journal of Marketing Research* 32 (3), 348–56.

Laird, Pamela Walker (2006), *Pull: Networking and Success since Benjamin Franklin.* Cambridge, Mass.: Harvard University Press.

Larson, Andrea (1992), "Network Dyads in Entrepreneurial Settings: A Study of the Governance of Exchange Relationships." *Administrative Science Quarterly* 37 (1), 76–104.

Latour, Bruno (1987), *Science in Action: How to Follow Scientists and Engineers through Society.* Cambridge, Mass.: Harvard University Press.

Lazarsfeld, Paul F., Bernard Berelson, and Hazel Gaudet (1944), *The People's Choice: How the Voter Makes Up His Mind in a Presidential Campaign.* New York, N.Y.: Duell, Sloan and Pearce.

Leblebici, Huseyin, Gerald R. Salancik, Anne Copay, and Tom King (1991), "Institutional Change and the Transformation of Interorganizational Fields: An Organizational History of the U.S. Radio Broadcasting Industry." *Administrative Science Quarterly* 36 (3), 333–63.

Lee, Nancy Howell (1969), *The Search for an Abortionist.* Chicago, Ill.: University of Chicago Press.

Leonard-Barton, Dorothy (1985), "Experts as Negative Opinion Leaders in the Diffusion of a Technological Innovation." *Journal of Consumer Research* 11 (4), 914–26.

Liebowitz, S. J., and Stephen E. Margolis (1990), "The Fable of the Keys." *Journal of Law and Economics* 33 (1), 1–25.

Liebowitz, S. J., and Stephen E. Margolis (1994), "Network Externality: An Uncommon Tragedy." *Journal of Economic Perspectives* 8 (2), 133–50.

Liebowitz, Stan J., and Stephen E. Margolis (1999), *Winners, Losers & Microsoft: Competition and Antitrust in High Technology.* Oakland, Calif.: Independent Institute.

Lilien, Gary L. (1994), "Marketing Models: Past, Present, and Future." In *Research Traditions in Marketing*, eds. Gilles Laurent, Gary L. Lilien, and Barnard Pras, 1–20. Boston, Mass.: Kluwer Academic Publishers.

Lilien, Gary L., Pamela D. Morrison, Kathleen Searls, Mary Sonnack, and Eric von Hippel (2002), "Performance Assessment of the Lead User Idea-Generation Process for New Product Development." *Management Science* 48 (8), 1042–59.

Lin, Nan (2001), *Social Capital: A Theory of Social Structure and Action.* Cambridge, U.K.: Cambridge University Press.

Linton, Ralph (1936), *The Study of Man: An Introduction*. New York, N.Y.: D. Appleton-Century.

Lodish, Leonard M., Magid Abraham, Stuart Kalmenson, Jeanne Livelsberger, Beth Lubetkin, Bruce Richardson, and Mary Ellen Stevens (1995a), "How T.V. Advertising Works: A Meta-analysis of 389 Real World Split Cable T.V. Advertising." *Journal of Marketing Research* 32 (2), 125–39.

Lodish, Leonard M., Magid M. Abraham, Jeanne Livelsberger, Beth Lubetkin, Bruce Richardson, and Mary Ellen Stevens (1995b), "A Summary of Fifty-Five In-Market Experimental Estimates of the Long-Term Effect of TV Advertising." *Marketing Science* 14 (3), G133–G140.

Lusch, Robert F. (1976), "Sources of Power: Their Impact on Intrachannel Conflict." *Journal of Marketing Research* 13 (4), 382–90.

Macaulay, Stewart (1963), "Non-Contractual Relations in Business: A Preliminary Study." *American Sociological Review* 28 (1), 55–67.

Macy, Michael W., and Robert Willer (2002), "From Factors to Actors: Computational Sociology and Agent-Based Modeling." *Annual Review of Sociology* 28, 143–66.

Madhavan, Ravindranath, Devi R. Gnyawali, and Jinyu He (2004), "Two's Company, Three's a Crowd? Triads in Cooperative-Competitive Networks." *Academy of Management Journal* 47 (6), 918–27.

Mansfield, Edwin (1961), "Technical Change and the Rate of Imitation." *Econometrica* 29, 741–66.

Markovsky, Barry, David Willer, and Travis Patton (1988), "Power Relations in Exchange Networks." *American Sociological Review* 53 (2), 220–36.

Marsden, Peter V. (1989), "Methods for the Characterization of Role Structures in Network Analysis." In *Research Methods in Social Network Analysis*, eds. Linton C. Freeman, Douglas R. White, and A. Kimball Romney, 489–530. Fairfax, Va.: George Mason University Press.

Marsden, Peter V. (1990), "Network Data and Measurement." *Annual Review of Sociology* 16, 435–63

Marsden, Peter V. (2005), "Recent Developments in Network Measurement." In *Models and Methods in Social Network Analysis*, eds. Peter J. Carrington, John Scott, and Stanley Wasserman, 8-30. Cambridge, U.K.: Cambridge University Press.

Marsden, Peter V., and Karen E. Campbell (1984), "Measuring Tie Strength." *Social Forces* 63 (2), 482–501.

Marsden, Peter V., and Noah E. Friedkin (1994), "Network Studies of Social Influence." In *Advances in Social Network Analysis: Research in the Social and Behavioral Sciences*, eds. Stanley Wasserman and Joseph Galaskiewicz, 3–25. Thousand Oaks, Calif.: Sage.

Martilla, John A. (1971), "Word-of-Mouth Communication in the Industrial Adoption Process." *Journal of Marketing Research* 8 (2), 173–8.

Martin, John Levi (2002), "Power, Authority, and the Constraint of Belief Systems." *American Journal of Sociology* 107 (4), 861–904.

Matthyssens, Paul, and Christophe Van den Bulte (1994), "Getting Closer and Nicer: Partnerships in the Supply Chain." *Long Range Planning* 27 (1), 72–83.

McAdam, Doug, and Ronnelle Paulsen (1993), "Specifying the Relationship Between Social Ties and Activism." *American Journal of Sociology* 99 (3), 640–67.

McGuire, Patrick, Mark Granovetter, and Michael Schwartz (1993), "Thomas Edison and the Social Construction of the Early Electricity Industry in America." In *Explorations in Economic Sociology*, ed. Richard Swedberg, 213–48. New York, N.Y.: Russell Sage Foundation.

McLean, Paul D. (1998), "A Frame Analysis of Favor Seeking in the Renaissance: Agency Networks and Political Culture." *American Journal of Sociology* 104 (1), 51–91.

McPherson, Miller, Lynn Smith-Lovin, and James M. Cook (2001), "Birds of a Feather: Homophily in Social Networks." *Annual Review of Sociology* 27, 415–44.

Merton, Robert K. (1949), "Patterns of Influence: A Study of Interpersonal Influence and Communications Behavior in a Local Community." In *Communications Research, 1948-1949*, eds. Paul F. Lazarsfeld and Frank N. Stanton, 180–219. New York, N.Y.: Harper & Brothers.

Merton, Robert K. (1968), *Social Theory and Social Structure*. 1968 enlarged edition. New York, N.Y.: Free Press.

Midgley, David F., Pamela D. Morrison, and John H. Roberts (1992), "The Effect of Network Structure in Industrial Diffusion Processes." *Research Policy* 21 (6), 533–52.

Milo, R., S. Shen-Orr, S. Itzkovitz, N. Kashtan, D. Chklovskii, and U. Alon (2002), "Network Motifs: Simple Building Blocks of Complex Networks." *Science* 298 (5594), 824–7.

Mitchell, J. Clyde (1969), "The Concept and Use of Social Networks." In *Social Networks in Urban Situations*, ed. J. Clyde Mitchell, 1–52. Manchester, U.K.: University of Manchester Press.

Mizruchi, Mark S., and Linda Brewster Stearns (2001), "Getting Deals Done: The Use of Social Networks in Bank Decision-Making." *American Sociological Review* 66 (5), 647–71.

Moenaert, Rudy K., and William E. Souder (1990), "An Information Transfer Model for Integrating Marketing and R&D Personnel in New Product Development Projects." *Journal of Product Innovation Management* 7 (2), 91–107.

Molm, Linda D., Theron M. Quist, and Phillip A. Wiseley (1994), "Imbalanced Structures, Unfair Strategies: Power and Justice in Social Exchange." *American Sociological Review* 59 (1), 98–121.

Molnár, Virág, and Michèle Lamont (2002), "Social Categorisation and Group Identification: How African-Americans Shape their Collective Identity through Consumption." In *Innovation by Demand: An Interdisciplinary Approach to the Study of Demand and its Role in Innovation*, eds. Andrew McMeekin, Ken Green, Mark Tomlinson, and Vivien Walsh, 88–111. Manchester, U.K.: Manchester University Press.

Money, R. Bruce, Mary C. Gilly, and John L. Graham (1998), "Explorations of National Culture and Word-of-Mouth Referral Behavior in the Purchase of Industrial Services in the United States and Japan." *Journal of Marketing* 62 (4), 76–87.

Montgomery, James D. (1996), "The Structure of Social Exchange Networks: A Game-Theoretic Reformulation of Blau's Model." *Sociological Methodology* 26, 193–225.

Montgomery, James D. (1998), "Toward a Role-Theoretic Conception of Embeddedness." *American Journal of Sociology* 104 (1), 92–125.

Moody, James (2001), "Race, School Integration, and Friendship Segregation in America." *American Journal of Sociology* 107 (3), 679–716.

Moody, James, and Douglas R. White (2003), "Structural Cohesion and Embeddedness: A Hierarchical Concept of Social Groups." *American Sociological Review* 68 (1), 103–27.

Moore, Geoffrey A. (1991), *Crossing the Chasm*. New York, N.Y.: HarperBusiness

Moorman, Christine, and Roland T. Rust (1999), "The Role of Marketing." *Journal of Marketing* 63 (Special Issue), 180–97.

Moriarty, Rowland T. (1983), *Industrial Buying Behavior: Concepts, Issues, and Applications*. Lexington, Mass.: Lexington Books.

Mudrack, Peter E. (1989), "Defining Group Cohesiveness: A Legacy of Confusion?" *Small Group Behavior* 20, 37–49.

Muniz, Albert M., Jr., and Thomas C. O'Guinn (2001), "Brand Community." *Journal of Consumer Research* 27 (4), 412–32.

Myers, James H., and Thomas S. Robertson (1972), "Dimensions of Opinion Leadership." *Journal of Marketing Research* 9 (1), 41–6.

Nadel, S.F. (1957), *Theory of Social Structure*. Glencoe, Ill.: Free Press.

Nahapiet, Janine, and Sumantra Ghoshal (1998), "Social Capital, Intellectual Capital, and the Organizational Advantage." *Academy of Management Review* 23 (2), 242–66.

Neslin, Scott A. (2002), *Sales Promotion*. Cambridge, Mass.: Marketing Science Institute.

Newcomb, Theodore Mead (1961), *The Acquaintance Process*. New York, N.Y.: Holt, Rinehart and Winston.

Newman, M. E. J. (2001), "The Structure of Scientific Collaboration Networks." *Proceedings of the National Academy of Sciences of the United States of America* 98 (2), 404–9.

Newman, M. E. J. (2002), "Assortative Mixing in Networks." *Physical Review Letters* 89 (20), 208701.

Newman, M.E.J. (2003), "Properties of Highly Clustered Networks." *Physical Review E*, 026121.

Newman, M. E. J., and Juyong Park (2003), "Why Social Networks Are Different from Other Types of Networks." *Physical Review E* 68, 036122.

Newman, Mark (2003), "The Structure and Function of Complex Networks." *SIAM Review* 45 (2), 167–256.

Newman, Mark, Albert-László Barabási, and Duncan J. Watts, eds. (2006), *The Structure and Dynamics of Networks*. Princeton, N.J.: Princeton University Press.

Obstfeld, David (2005), "Social Networks, the Tertius Iungens Orientation, and Involvement in Innovation." *Administrative Science Quarterly* 50 (1), 100–30.

Ohtsuki, Hisashi, Christoph Hauert, Erez Lieberman, and Martin A. Nowak (2006), "A Simple Rule for the Evolution of Cooperation on Graphs and Social Networks." *Nature* 441, 502–5.

Park, C. Whan, and V. Parker Lessig (1977), "Students and Housewives: Differences in Susceptibility to Reference Group Influence." *Journal of Consumer Research* 4 (2), 102–10.

Perry-Smith, Jill E. (2006), "Social Yet Creative: The Role of Social Relationships in Facilitating Individual Creativity." *Academy of Management Journal* 49 (1), 85–101.

Podolny, Joel M. (1993), "A Status-based Model of Market Competition." *American Journal of Sociology* 98 (4), 829–72.

Podolny, Joel M. (2005), *Status Signals: A Sociological Study of Market Competition*. Princeton, N.J.: Princeton University Press.

Portes, Alejandro (1998), "Social Capital: Its Origins and Applications in Modern Sociology." *Annual Review of Sociology* 22, 1–24.

Portes, Alejandro, and Julia Sensenbrenner (1993), "Embeddedness and Immigration: Notes on the Social Determinants of Economic Action." *American Journal of Sociology* 98 (6), 1320–50.

Powell, Walter W., Kenneth W. Koput, and Laurel Smith-Doerr (1996), "Interorganizational Collaboration and the Locus of Innovation: Networks of Learning in Biotechnology." *Administrative Science Quarterly* 41 (1), 116–45.

Powell, Walter W., Kenneth W. Koput, Douglas R. White, and Jason Owen-Smith (2005), "Network Dynamics and Field Evolution: The Growth of Interorganizational Collaboration in the Life Sciences." *American Journal of Sociology* 110 (4), 1132–1205.

Putnam, Robert D. (2000), *Bowling Alone: The Collapse and Revival of American Community*. New York, N.Y.: Simon & Schuster.

Ragas, Matthew W., and Bolivar J. Bueno (2002), *The Power of Cult Branding: How 9 Magnetic Brands Turned Customers into Loyal Followers (and Yours Can Too)*. New York, N.Y.: Random House.

Raider, Holly, and David J. Krackhardt (2002), "Intraorganizational Networks." In *Blackwell Companion to Organizations*, ed. Joel A.C. Baum, 58–74. Oxford, U.K.: Blackwell.

Raub, Werner, and Jeroen Weesie (1990), "Reputation and Efficiency in Social Interactions: An Example of Network Effects." *American Journal of Sociology* 96 (3), 626–54.

Reagans, Ray, and Bill McEvily (2003), "Network Structure and Knowledge Transfer: The Effects of Cohesion and Range." *Administrative Science Quarterly* 48 (2), 240–67.

Reagans, Ray, and Ezra Zuckerman (2001), "Networks, Diversity, and Productivity: The Social Capital of Corporate R&D Teams." *Organization Science* 12 (4), 502–17.

Reagans, Ray, Ezra Zuckerman, and Bill McEvily (2004), "How to Make the Team: Social Networks vs. Demography as Criteria for Designing Effective Teams." *Administrative Science Quarterly* 49 (1), 101–33.

Reingen, Peter H., Brian L. Foster, Jacqueline Johnson Brown, and Stephen B. Seidman (1984), "Brand Congruence in Interpersonal Relations: A Social Network Analysis." *Journal of Consumer Research* 11 (3), 771–84.

Reingen, Peter H., and Jerome B. Kernan (1986), "Analysis of Referral Networks in Marketing—Methods and Illustration." *Journal of Marketing Research* 23 (4), 370–8.

Rindfleisch, Aric, and Christine Moorman (2001), "The Acquisition and Utilization of Information in New Product Alliances: A Strength-of-Ties Perspective." *Journal of Marketing* 65 (2), 1–18.

Riskey, Dwight R. (1997), "How T.V. Advertising Works: An Industry Response." *Journal of Marketing Research* 34 (2), 292–3.

Roberts, John H., and Glen L. Urban (1988), "Modeling Multiattribute Utility, Risk, and Belief Dynamics for New Consumer Durable Brand Choice." *Management Science* 34, 167–85.

Robins, Garry, and Philippa Pattison (2001), "Random Graph Models for Temporal Processes in Social Networks." *Journal of Mathematical Sociology* 25 (1), 5–41.

Robins, Garry, and Philippa Pattison (2005), "Interdependencies and Social Proceses: Dependence Graphs and Generalized Dependence Structures." In *Models and Methods in Social Network Analysis*, eds. Peter J. Carrington, John Scott, and Stanley Wasserman, 194–214. Cambridge, U.K.: Cambridge University Press.

Rogers, Everett M. (2003), *Diffusion of Innovations,* 5th ed. New York, N.Y.: Free Press.

Rogers, Everett M., and D. Lawrence Kincaid (1981), *Communication Networks: Toward a New Paradigm for Research.* New York, N.Y.: Free Press.

Ronchetto, John R., Jr., Michael D. Hutt, and Peter H. Reingen (1989), "Embedded Influence Patterns in Organizational Buying Systems." *Journal of Marketing* 53 (4), 51–63.

Rosen, Emanuel (2000), *The Anatomy of Buzz: How to Create Word of Mouth Marketing.* New York, N.Y.: Doubleday.

Rowley, Tim, Dean Behrens, and David Krackhardt (2000), "Redundant Governance Structures: An Analysis of Structural and Relational Embeddedness in the Steel and Semiconductor Industries." *Strategic Management Journal* 21, 369–86.

Salzman, Marian, Ira Matathia, and Ann O'Reilly (2003), *Buzz: Harness the Power of Influence and Create Demand.* Hoboken, N.J.: Wiley.

Shaw, Steven J. (1965), "Behavioral Science Offers Fresh Insights on New Product Acceptance." *Journal of Marketing* 29 (1), 9–13.

Silk, Alvin J. (1966), "Overlap among Self-designated Opinion Leaders: A Study of Selected Dental Products and Services." *Journal of Marketing Research* 3 (3), 255–9.

Silverman, George (2001), *The Secrets of Word-of-Mouth Marketing: How to Trigger Exponential Sales Through Runaway Word of Mouth.* New York, N.Y.: AMACOM.

Simmel, Georg (1950), *The Sociology of Georg Simmel,* ed. Kurt H. Wolff. New York, N.Y.: Free Press.

Simmel, Georg (1955), *Conflict and The Web of Group-Affiliations.* New York, N.Y.: Free Press.

Sirsi, Ajay K., James C. Ward, and Peter H. Reingen (1996), "Microcultural Analysis of Variation in Sharing of Causal Reasoning about Behavior." *Journal of Consumer Research* 22 (4), 345–72.

Sivadas, Eugene, and F. Robert Dwyer (2000), "An Examination of Organizational Factors Influencing New Product Success in Internal and Alliance-Based Processes." *Journal of Marketing* 64 (January), 31–49.

Skvoretz, John, and David Willer (1993), "Exclusion and Power: A Test of Four Theories of Power in Exchange Networks." *American Sociological Review* 58 (6), 801–18.

Smith, Douglas K., and Robert C. Alexander (1988), *Fumbling the Future: How Xerox Invented, then Ignored, the First Personal Computer.* New York, N.Y.: W. Morrow.

Smith, Sandra Susan (2005), "'Don't Put My Name on It': Social Capital Activation and Job-Finding Assistance among the Black Urban Poor." *American Journal of Sociology* 111 (1), 1–57.

Smith-Doerr, Laurel, and Walter W. Powell (2005), "Networks and Economic Life." In *Handbook of Economic Sociology*, eds. Neil J. Smelser and Richard Swedberg, 379–402. Princeton, N.J.: Princeton University Press.

Snijders, Tom A.B. (2001), "The Statistical Evaluation of Social Network Dynamics." *Sociological Methodology* 31, 361–95.

Snow, David A., Louis A. Zurcher Jr., and Sheldon Ekland-Olson (1980), "Social Networks and Social Movements: A Microstructural Approach to Differential Recruitment." *American Sociological Review* 45 (5), 787–801.

Stafford, James E. (1966), "Effects of Group Influences on Consumer Brand Preferences." *Journal of Marketing Research* 3 (1), 68–75.

Stiglitz, Joseph E. (1990), "Peer Monitoring and Credit Markets." *World Bank Economic Review* 4 (3), 351–66.

Stuart, Toby E., Ha Hoang, and Ralph C. Hybels (1999), "Interorganizational Endorsements and the Performance of Entrepreneurial Ventures." *Administrative Science Quarterly* 44 (2), 315–49.

Summers, John O. (1971), "Generalized Change Agents and Innovativeness." *Journal of Marketing Research* 8 (3), 313–6.

Szulanski, Gabriel (1997), "Exploring Internal Stickiness: Impediments to the Transfer of Best Practice within the Firm." *Strategic Management Journal* 17 (Winter Special Issue), 27–43.

Szulanski, Gabriel, Rossella Cappetta, and Robert J. Jensen (2004), "When and How Trustworthiness Matters: Knowledge Transfer and the Moderating Effect of Causal Ambiguity." *Organization Science* 15 (5), 600–13.

Thibaut, John W., and Harold Kelly (1959), *The Social Psychology of Groups*. New York, N.Y.: Wiley.

Thirtle, Colin G., and Vernon W. Ruttan (1987), *The Role of Demand and Supply in the Generation and Diffusion of Technical Change*. Chur, U.K.: Harwood Academic.

Travers, Jeffrey, and Stanley Milgram (1969), "An Experimental Study of the Small World Problem." *Sociometry* 32 (4), 425–43.

Turow, Joseph (1997), *Breaking up America: Advertisers and the New Media World*. Chicago, Ill.: University of Chicago Press.

Tushman, Michael L., and Ralph Katz (1980), "External Communication and Project Performance: An Investigation into the Role of Gatekeepers." *Management Science* 26 (11), 1071–85.

Tushman, Michael L., and Elaine Romanelli (1983), "Uncertainty, Social Location, and Influence in Decision Making: A Sociometric Analysis." *Management Science* 29 (1), 12–23.

Urban, Glen L., and John R. Hauser (2004), "'Listening-In' to Find and Explore New Combinations of Customer Needs." *Journal of Marketing* 68 (2), 72–87.

Üstüner, Tuba, and David Godes (2006), "Better Sales Networks." *Harvard Business Review* 84 (7/8), 102–12.

Uzzi, Brian (1997), "Social Structure and Competition in Interfirm Networks: The Paradox of Embeddedness." *Administrative Science Quarterly* 42 (1), 35–67.

Uzzi, Brian, and Ryon Lancaster (2003), "Relational Embeddedness and Learning: The Case of Bank Loan Managers and Their Clients." *Management Science* 49 (4), 383–99.

Uzzi, Brian, and Ryon Lancaster (2004), "Embeddedness and Price Formation in the Corporate Law Market." *American Sociological Review* 69 (3), 319–44.

Uzzi, Brian, and Jarrett Spiro (2005), "Collaboration and Creativity: The Small World Problem." *American Journal of Sociology* 111 (2), 447–504.

Valente, Thomas W., Beth R. Hoffman, Annamara Ritt-Olson, Kara Lichtman, and C. Anderson Johnson (2003), "Effects of a Social-network Method for Group Assignment Strategies on Peer-led Tobacco Prevention Programs in Schools." *American Journal of Public Health* 93, 1837–43.

Van den Bulte, Christophe (1994), "Metaphor at Work." In *Research Traditions in Marketing*, eds. Gilles Laurent, Gary L. Lilien, and Bernard Pras, 405–25. Boston, Mass.: Kluwer Academic Publishers.

Van den Bulte, Christophe, and Yogesh Joshi (2007), "New Product Diffusion with Influentials and Imitators." *Marketing Science,* in press.

Van den Bulte, Christophe, and Gary L. Lilien (2001), "*Medical Innovation* Revisited: Social Contagion versus Marketing Effort." *American Journal of Sociology* 106 (5), 1409–35.

Van den Bulte, Christophe, and Rudy K. Moenaert (1998), "The Effect of R&D Team Co-location on Communication Patterns among R&D, Marketing and Manufacturing." *Management Science* 44 (11), S1–S18.

Van den Bulte, Christophe, and Stefan Stremersch (2004), "Social Contagion and Income Heterogeneity in New Product Diffusion: A Meta-analytic Test." *Marketing Science* 23 (4), 530–44.

van Duijn, Marijtje A. J., Jooske T. van Busschbach, and Tom A. B. Snijders (1999), "Multilevel Analysis of Personal Networks as Dependent Variables." *Social Networks* 21 (2), 187–210.

van Waterschoot, Walter, and Christophe Van den Bulte (1992), "The 4P Classification of the Marketing Mix Revisited." *Journal of Marketing* 56 (4), 83–93.

Verbeke, Willem, and Stefan Wuyts (2007), "Moving in Social Circles—Social Circle Membership and Performance Implications." *Journal of Organizational Behavior,* in press.

Walker, Michael E., Stanley Wasserman, and Barry Wellman (1994), "Statistical Models for Social Support Networks." In *Advances in Social Network Analysis: Research in the Social and Behavioral Sciences*, eds. Stanley Wasserman and Joseph Galaskiewicz, 53–78. Thousand Oaks, Calif.: Sage.

Ward, James C., and Peter H. Reingen (1990), "Sociocognitive Analysis of Group Decision Making among Consumers." *Journal of Consumer Research* 17 (3), 245–62.

Wasserman, Stanley, and Katherine Faust (1994), *Social Network Analysis: Methods and Applications*. Cambridge, U.K.: Cambridge University Press.

Wathne, Kenneth H., and Jan B. Heide (2004), "Relationship Governance in a Supply Chain Network." *Journal of Marketing* 68 (1), 73–89.

Watts, Duncan J. (2002), "A Simple Model of Global Cascades on Random Networks," *Proceedings of the National Academy of Sciences of the United States of America* 99 (9), 5766–71.

Watts, Duncan J. (2003), *Six Degrees: The Science of a Connected Age*. New York, N.Y.: W. W. Norton & Company.

Watts, Duncan J. (2004), "The 'New' Science of Networks." *Annual Review of Sociology* 30, 243–70.

Watts, Duncan J., Peter Sheridan Dodds, and M.E. J. Newman (2002), "Identity and Search in Social Networks." *Science* 296 (5571), 1302–5.

Watts, Duncan J., and Steven H. Strogatz (1998), "Collective Dynamics of 'Small-World' Networks." *Nature* 393, 440–2.

Weber, Max (1968 [1921]), *Economy and Society*. Translated by G. Roth and C. Wittich. Totowa, N.J.: Bedminster Press.

Webster, Frederick E., Jr. (1970), "Informal Communication in Industrial Markets." *Journal of Marketing Research* 7 (2), 186–9.

Weimann, Gabriel (1994), *The Influentials: People who Influence People*. Albany, N.Y.: State University of New York Press.

Wellman, Barry, and Scot Wortley (1990), "Different Strokes from Different Folks: Community Ties and Social Support." *American Journal of Sociology* 96 (3), 558–88.

Westphal, James D., Ranjay Gulati, and Stephen M. Shortell (1997), "Customization and Conformity? An Institutional and Network Perspective on the Content and Consequences of TQM Adoption." *Administrative Science Quarterly* 42 (2), 366–94.

White, Douglas R., and Frank Harary (2001), "The Cohesiveness of Blocks in Social Networks: Node Connectivity and Conditional Density." *Sociological Methodology* 31, 305–59.

White, Harrison C. (1970), "Search Parameters for the Small World Problem." *Social Forces* 49 (2), 259–64.

Wilkinson, Ian F. (1976), "An Exploration of Methodologies for Detecting Subgroups, Subsystems and Cliques of Firms in Distribution Channels." *Journal of the Academy of Marketing Science* 4 (2), 539–53.

Williamson, Oliver E. (1975), *Markets and Hierarchies: Analysis and Antitrust Implications*. New York, N.Y.: Free Press.

Williamson, Oliver E. (1985). *The Economic Institutions of Capitalism: Firms, Markets, Relational Contracting.* New York, N.Y.: Free Press.

Williamson, Oliver E. (1996). *The Mechanisms of Governance.* Oxford, U.K.: Oxford University Press.

Wind, Jerry, and Vijay Mahajan (1997), "Issues and Opportunities in New Product Development: An Introduction to the Special Issue." *Journal of Marketing Research* 34 (1), 1–12.

Wish, Myron (1976), "Comparisons among Multidimensional Structures of Interpersonal Relations." *Multivariate Behavioral Research* 11 (3), 297–324.

Witt, Robert E., and Grady D. Bruce (1970), "Purchase Decisions and Group Influence." *Journal of Marketing Research* 7 (4), 533–5.

Wuyts, Stefan, Shantanu Dutta, and Stefan Stremersch (2004), "Portfolios of Interfirm Agreements in Technology-Intensive Markets: Consequences for Innovation and Profitability." *Journal of Marketing* 68 (2), 88–100.

Wuyts, Stefan, and Inge Geyskens (2005), "The Formation of Buyer-Supplier Relationships: Detailed Contract Drafting and Close Partner Selection." *Journal of Marketing* 69 (4), 103–17.

Wuyts, Stefan, Stefan Stremersch, Christophe Van den Bulte, and Philip Hans Franses (2004), "Vertical Marketing Systems for Complex Products: A Triadic Perspective." *Journal of Marketing Research* 41 (4), 479–87.

Zeithaml, Valarie A., and A. Parasuraman (2004), *Service Quality.* Cambridge, Mass.: Marketing Science Institute.

ABOUT THE AUTHORS

Christophe Van den Bulte is Associate Professor of Marketing at the Wharton School of the University of Pennsylvania, where he has been teaching since 1997.

His research interests include new product diffusion, social networks, and business-to-business marketing. He has published several articles on these topics in journals such as the *American Journal of Sociology, Journal of Marketing, Journal of Marketing Research, Management Science,* and *Marketing Science.* He serves on the editorial boards of the *International Journal of Research in Marketing, Journal of Business-to-Business Marketing, Journal of Marketing Research,* and *Marketing Science.*

Van den Bulte has consulted with organizations including Bristol-Myers Squibb, DuPont, Monsanto, the National Institute of Standards and Technology, and the RAND Corporation, and has spoken at a number of executive education seminars and other meetings for companies including LG Electronics, Philip Morris, and Pfizer.

He holds an undergraduate degree in applied economics from the University of Antwerp, Belgium, and a Ph.D. in business administration from The Pennsylvania State University.

Stefan Wuyts is Assistant Professor of Marketing at Tilburg University, The Netherlands, where he has been teaching since 2005. His research interests include channel relationships and alliances, innovation, social networks, and business-to-business marketing. His work in these areas has appeared in journals such as the *Journal of Marketing* and *Journal of Marketing Research.* He serves on the editorial board of the *International Journal of Research in Marketing.*

Wuyts has received grants from diverse research institutions including the Marketing Science Institute, the Institute for the Study of Business Markets, and the Netherlands Organisation for Scientific Research. He has consulted with and spoken at meetings at several companies, including SAP and Nexans.

He holds an undergraduate degree in business engineering from the University of Louvain (Katholieke Universiteit Leuven), Belgium, a master's degree in marketing from the Vlerick Management School, Belgium, and a Ph.D. in business economics from Erasmus University Rotterdam, The Netherlands. His doctoral dissertation was awarded by the Dutch Royal Society for Economics as the best dissertation defended at an Economics Faculty in The Netherlands in 2003 and 2004.

ABOUT MSI

Founded in 1961, the Marketing Science Institute is a learning organization dedicated to bridging the gap between marketing science theory and business practice. MSI currently brings together executives from approximately 70 sponsoring corporations with leading researchers from over 100 universities worldwide.

As a nonprofit institution, MSI financially supports academic research for the development—and practical translation—of leading-edge marketing knowledge on topics of importance to business. Issues of key importance to business performance are identified by the Board of Trustees, which represents MSI corporations and the academic community. MSI supports studies by academics on these issues and disseminates the results through conferences and workshops, as well as through its publications series.

Related MSI Working Papers

Report No.

06-124 "The Role of Expert versus Social Opinion Leaders in New Product Adoption" by Jacob Goldenberg, Donald R. Lehmann, Daniella Shidlovski, and Michal Master Barak

06-119 "The Impact of Marketing-induced versus Word-of-Mouth Customer Acquisition on Customer Equity" by Julian Villanueva, Shijin Yoo, and Dominique M. Hanssens

06-118 "Measuring the Value of Word-of-Mouth and Its Impact in Consumer Communities" by Paul Dwyer

06-111 "What Drives Word-of-Mouth? The Roles of Product Originality and Usefulness" by Sarit Moldovan, Jacob Goldenberg, and Amitava Chattopadhyay

05-112 "Brand Concept Maps: A Methodology for Identifying Brand Association Networks" by Deborah Roedder John, Barbara Loken, Kyeong-Heui Kim, and Alokparna Basu Monga

05-105 "Standard-Scape: An Agent-based Model of Competition in Markets with Network Externalities" by Judy K. Frels, James A. Reggia, and Debra Heisler

05-100 "First-mover Advantage on the Internet: Real or Virtual?" by Rajan Varadarajan, Manjit S. Yadav, and Venkatesh Shankar

02-118 "The Social Capital of the Top Marketing Team, Inter-firm Market Learning Capability, and Business Performance: A Test of a Mediating Model" by Kwaku Atuahene-Gima

02-108 "What Is the True Value of a Lost Customer?" by John E. Hogan, Katherine N. Lemon, and Barak Libai

02-106 "From Density to Destiny: Using Spatial Analysis for Early Prediction of New Product Success" by Tal Garber, Jacob Goldenberg, Barak Libai, and Eitan Muller